YOUR
RIGHT JOB
RIGHT NOW

Unconventional Wisdom, Unbelievable Results
from
My Boss June

YOUR
RIGHT JOB
RIGHT NOW

Unconventional Wisdom, Unbelievable Results
from
My Boss June

by Brian Golter

AMBASSADOR INTERNATIONAL
GREENVILLE, SOUTH CAROLINA & BELFAST, NORTHERN IRELAND

www.ambassador-international.com

Your Right Job, Right Now

Unconventional Wisdom, Unbelievable Results from My Boss June

www.mybossjune.com

Printed in the United States of America

ISBN 978-1-932307-45-0

Cover Design & Page Layout by David Siglin of A&E Media

AMBASSADOR INTERNATIONAL
Emerald House
427 Wade Hampton Blvd.
Greenville, SC 29609, USA
www.ambassador-international.com

AMBASSADOR PUBLICATIONS
Providence House
Ardenlee Street
Belfast, BT6 8QJ, Northern Ireland, UK
www.ambassador-productions.com

The colophon is a trademark of Ambassador

Editors: Vicki Huffman, Patricia McMahon

Table of Contents

CLUB HOLLYWOOD

2410 MISSION ST. • SAN FRANCISCO

presents

June Gregory

Singing Sensation

Dedicated to June Gregory, in loving memory.

Prologue

When I wrote this book in 2008, I had in mind those rare individuals who want to see their careers as an opportunity to transform themselves. To overcome their deep-rooted fears and inadequacies, and become the man or woman they had always dreamed of being. It was a book about turning fear into courage, mistrust into trust and inadequacy into confidence.

But as the saying goes, "that was then and this is now". Since the time I completed this manuscript, we have entered into one of the most difficult job markets in modern history. This book is no longer for rare individuals. It has become a survival guide for the new job market. Understanding how to bring your absolute best to the job market is no longer a luxury. It has become a necessity.

The old rules simply no longer apply. If you're looking for a job, it's no longer enough to get on the computer, send out your résumé and expect to get a job. The days of just "showing up" to the interview and getting an attractive offer are over.

Quite simply, if you are experiencing a lack of motivation, enthusiasm or confidence, you are not going to find the job you want.

No, faking won't help you either. In this market, employers have their choice of hundreds of candidates. Of course, they will eliminate people on the traditional criteria: by experience, skills and salary. But what most job seekers don't realize is just how large a role expectations, confidence, risk-taking and attitude play in getting the job they want. They play a larger role than education and experience. This has always been true. Today's serious candidates have to pay attention to those deep places in themselves: those places that determine how other people experience them. The days of covering up the real you and still getting what you want are slowly but surely coming to an end.

For those of you willing to do the work of overcoming your fears and inadequacies, there is a silver lining. And what a wonderful silver lining it is! It's truly a new day in which you can reach for what you know is true and rewarding. A day in which you can no longer get away with, or be rewarded for, the very things you don't like about yourself. A day when you can become the man or woman you have always wanted to be.

For those of you who refuse to take up this challenge, it could just be the death sentence of your career.

It's time to get real and dig deep. To use the adversity you are experiencing to become so honest with yourself, so humble, that you will get the right job, right now.

Introduction

This is a story about my boss June. I worked for June for 20 years, from 1983 until her death in 2003. A former torch singer with the Big Bands of the late '40s and '50s, this five-foot, 200-pound spitfire owned a highly successful headhunting firm in California's Silicon Valley where I joined her as a recruiter. I later became her apprentice in the art of career counseling. Her counseling could more appropriately be termed "career and life choice butt-kicking." Few left June's presence unscathed, but nearly all appreciated her straightforward, no-holds-barred approach to finding fulfillment in life and work. She changed lives. She lived large. She loved larger.

It was always a great mystery, to both June and to me why she hired me in the first place. June had exposed my secret in our first meeting. After a childhood of abuse and neglect, I lived behind a facade, arrogantly hiding my lack of self-worth. June, who was always certain about her motivation and an expert at hiring decisions, saw right through me. Yet she could never clearly explain why she gave me the job. When asked, she shook her head and said, "For the life of me, I really don't know. He didn't have any of the qualities I look for."

She went so far as to call me a liar during our first encounter. As for me, there was no common sense in accepting the position. It wasn't the job, industry, salary or commute I wanted. In fact, there was no salary. It was commission only at a time in my life when I desperately needed a guaranteed income. Added to that, she exposed my fears and insecurities on day one. What else was she capable of uncovering?

It wasn't until I started writing this book that the mystery began to make sense. If June could take me, the guy no one in their right mind would want to hire, and transform me into the man I always wanted to be, then she could do it for anyone. I don't know you, but as you are about to read, chances are my problems were bigger, deeper and more complex than any obstacles you are currently facing in your career or life.

This is not a book about how I became successful. It is a book about how a great woman – an answer to prayer – saved me from a life of professional, financial and emotional misery. She gave me my life back. As you begin to read these chapters, I believe she will do the same for you.

"Ouch, That Hurt"

You know the experience. You have something on your mind about someone and you would like to tell the person, but you just can't. It might be a friend, family member or co-worker. It might be someone you just met or someone you have known your entire life. Whenever you see that person, you have thoughts like: he's too bossy; she talks too much; why is her hair like that; he doesn't look at me when he speaks; she can never seem to make up her mind; he's just irritating. You know the kind of thoughts I'm talking about. We have them all the time. Wouldn't you love to be able to tell people the obvious things they are doing that bother you? But you can't. That would be mean, critical and judgmental. You don't want to hurt their feelings. And what if you're wrong? No, it's better just to play it safe and not say anything at all. You don't want to be confrontational. Besides, does it really bother you that much? For the sake of keeping the peace, you keep your thoughts to yourself.

Unless you're June! She made it her business to tell people the negative things they were doing. The things everyone else was thinking about them, but no one else would say. Unlike the mean-spirited schoolmate, uncle or parent, she was able to communicate negative messages in a manner that most people could hear, learn from and even appreciate.

To come face to face with your greatest weakness and then suddenly to discover your courage and passion; that is the effect June had on those who met her. And that is the effect she continues to have, even after her death, on those of us who knew her well.

In fact, I can hear her right now: "Enough explanation, Brian. Just bring your readers into your office and let them sit in on an interview. Who's your next interview? His name is Mark? Okay, interview Mark and let everybody see what I taught you."

"But, June, you don't understand. Before I can invite them into an interview, I have to set the stage. I need to explain to them how you worked, about how we met, about your employment agency and why it was so successful. I just can't throw readers into the middle of an interview. It won't make sense to them."

"They're smart. If you would stop explaining, they could figure it out on their own. After all these years, and even after having a successful agency of your own, you're still learning how to trust people, aren't you? Isn't this book about learning how to trust? I suggest you do it rather than just talk about it."

Well, then, welcome to the world of my boss June.

"Rescue is the constant pattern of God's activity."
Francis Frangipane

Mark

"Tell me about your ideal job," I asked.

"Wow, my ideal job. I've been thinking a lot about that lately, and I can tell you that what I'm looking for is in one of three areas. It would be working in deal development for a venture capital firm, or product marketing in a start-up environment or maybe, I'm not really sure, but I might consider a product-marketing position in a mid-sized social networking company that is growing. It would have to be growing very fast. I might also consider a position that paid really well," Mark droned on.

"Let me ask you another question," I said, interrupting him. "Let's say I was able to find you one of the exact opportunities you just described. What would you do if, after being on the job for three months, you discovered the leadership of the company was unethical in their business dealings?"

"Oh, I wouldn't stand for it! I would leave. I'm not going to work for a company like that," he insisted.

"Are you telling me that after finding your ideal position you would leave it, just like that, in three months?"

Mark looked puzzled. He stared blankly at me as though I had asked him a question in some foreign language. At twenty-six he had two years of high-tech marketing under his belt and had just graduated with a MBA from Stanford. It was evident that he had high energy, was extremely bright, ambitious and ready to take on the world. Despite his intelligence, education and time spent contemplating his career, he had absolutely no idea how to answer my question.

He paused. With hesitation and looking completely bewildered he said, "Yes, I guess that's what I'm saying."

"What does that tell you about your ideal job?" I asked.

"I guess it tells me that it's not so ideal. To be honest, I hadn't thought about it from that perspective."

"Mark, what I'm about to tell you is going to be a complete 180-degree change in how you think about your career. I'm going to need your attention here. Do I have it?"

"Yes," he replied earnestly. The expression on Mark's face revealed that he was perplexed.

"The single most important aspect of any job is the quality of your relationship with the leadership of the company. What your answer revealed is that if you had the duties, title, salary, industry, promises of growth or any other desire in your wildest dreams, but didn't respect the leadership you worked for, you wouldn't be happy in your job. In fact, to your credit, you not only wouldn't be happy, you would feel compelled to leave what appeared to be the perfect position."

"I never looked at it that way."

While Mark was still considering my feedback, I glanced down at the calendar on my desk. The day was February 22, 2008 – four years to the day since June had passed away. The four years following her death had been remarkable. Continuing her legacy, I had opened the doors to my own search firm. My daughter Jessy helped me start it. From day one the firm had been a runaway success. We had put together a great team and were doing three times more business than we had thought possible. Although we were the new kid on the block, we had already established ourselves as one of the premier headhunting firms in the Silicon Valley.

I had also met and married Kim, the woman of my dreams. Because of the success of the business, we were able to afford to buy our ideal home in Kim's favorite town.

But more than the success of the business or meeting Kim, I had become the man I had always dreamed of becoming – the person I knew, even at my lowest point, that I was capable of being. All the hard work and involvement June had poured into me was paying off in ways I could never have imagined. She had taken a scared, angry and mistrustful boy of 23 and turned him into a man. The same man who was now trying to help Mark navigate his career path. I turned my attention back to the interview.

"The deepest need and desire in your work life is to work for leadership that inspires and respects you. That's not only the deepest need and desire of *your* work life; it's *everyone's* deepest need and desire. No matter how much money we make or what great things we accomplish, it is our relationship with the leadership of the company that will most greatly influence our fulfillment, growth and pride of accomplishment," I explained.

"That's a very different way of looking at my career," he said. The look of confusion was beginning to leave his face.

"Do you remember the movie *The Matrix*?" I asked.

"Yes, I really liked it."

"Do you remember the part when Neo has to decide whether to take the red pill or the blue pill?"

"Yes, I remember."

"Well, this is your red pill/blue pill moment. Take the blue pill and you will spend the rest of your career in the 'Matrix.' Like all the other masses of people, you will believe the way to success is found through chasing the right title, responsibilities, money, industry, promises of growth, great commute, early retirement, etc. This is a world where needs and desires are never really met, where what you have is never enough, where you find yourself stuck in one of two extremes: a constant unfulfilled striving for more or a passionless resignation that 'this is all there is.'"

"That sounds awful! What if I choose the red pill?" Mark asked.

"Take the red pill and you will enter a very different world. The world outside the 'Matrix' where the quality of your work life is greatly determined by the level of integrity and business skills of the leadership you work for. A world where your fulfillment and growth is real because it is based on a meaningful, ongoing relationship, a relationship that challenges and supports your deepest needs and desires, a relationship that brings out the best in you and makes you feel alive. Once you take the red pill, everything in your career will change."

I looked over at our recruiter, Maggie, who was sitting across the conference table from Mark. She had been so quiet I had almost forgotten she was in the room. Maggie had just started working for me the previous month. She was very excited about her interview with Mark. She felt that he was a highly placeable candidate. After a short time alone with him, she had come into my office asking if I would meet him and give her my opinion. For some reason, she looked more confused with what I told him than Mark did. I gave her a quick smile to reassure her. Her silence and apprehension reminded me of how I used to sit in on June's interviews – constantly worried and completely confused.

I turned my attention back to Mark, who seemed to be finding his bearings.

"Okay, I'm getting this," he said as if he had just put the pieces of a puzzle together or solved some great crime. "The last company I worked for had a very cool product. Because of that everyone thought that it must be a great company to work for. That is everyone except the employees. The company was so poorly managed that no one was happy. The two guys who founded the company were great engineers, but they didn't know anything about running a company. Everyone just kind of did what they thought they were supposed to do. There was no real direction."

"That sounds like a very frustrating environment."

"It was. I was miserable. So was everyone else. But are you really saying that I shouldn't base my job search on the industry or the responsibilities?"

"No, I'm not saying that they don't matter entirely. I am saying that, in the big picture, they don't matter nearly as much as you have been trained to believe."

Again Mark looked confused.

"Here's another metaphor that will help make this clear. Do you remember in your school years taking a class in a subject that you were really excited about only to find that the professor was a dud?"

"Yeah, I had a class like that," Mark said smiling.

"As the semester went by, what happened to your interest level in the subject?"

"It went down. Way down."

"What about your motivational level or desire to learn?"

"I didn't even want to go. I found ways to skip the lectures and just take the exams."

"Did you enjoy anything about the experience?"

"No. The class was in anthropology, which at the time was my favorite subject. I was even thinking of declaring it as my major. But after that class I changed my mind. The professor was really awful. He was boring. I don't even think *he* wanted to be there."

"Now, conversely, did you ever take a class in a subject you were not the least bit interested in only to discover that the professor was inspiring?"

"Yes, it was a class in ancient history," Mark said enthusiastically. "Since high school I hated going to history classes. I just never found them interesting. But this class turned out to be my favorite. The teacher was the coolest guy. He would describe past events as if you were actually there. He would literally stand in front of the class and act out these scenes from ancient history as if it was happening right there in the room. He managed to make everything fascinating. He also took a lot of personal interest in how the students were doing. You could tell that he really cared. I loved that class!"

"You see," I said, "the teacher, not your level of interest or passion for the subject matter is what most greatly determined your desire to learn, your growth and your enjoyment of the class."

"You're right. I even changed the whole direction of my studies because of one very lousy professor. On the other hand, even though I've been out of college for a while, I still find myself picking up a book on ancient history just for the fun of it."

"Now imagine for a moment that you could have gone through your entire school experience selecting courses solely on the quality of the teacher. Instead of taking classes based on the school's requirements for graduation, you could choose courses taught solely by your favorite teachers. How would you have felt about that?"

"That would have been very cool," he replied.

"Then I have some very good news to tell you about your career: you get to pick the teacher. You don't have to take any required courses from teachers you don't like, don't respect or find uninspiring. If you set your mind to it, you can find the very best leaders and spend your time in their classrooms learning, growing and enjoying yourself."

Mark didn't say anything. He sat there for a moment contemplating this. His body language was beginning to change. He was calming down, sitting back more relaxed in his chair. His shoulders were noticeably less tense. He was becoming more comfortable – a sure indication that the red pill was taking effect.

"Yes, it would be great to work for a company that had great leadership. Even at the last company I worked for; I knew that I was in the wrong place. But how can I tell if a company has great leadership in an interview? That seems impossible to me."

Maggie jumped in to tell Mark what she had recently learned about discerning the quality of leadership in a single interview. She was doing a pretty good job. As she spoke, my thoughts drifted back to my first interview with June almost 25 years earlier.

The Fearless Torch Singer

I noticed her eyes first. She had dark eyes that, in one moment, would light up with the most infectious joy I had ever seen and, in the next moment, would change to what could only be described as a fierce, menacing look. Despite – or maybe because of – the look in her eyes, I found myself feeling completely comfortable in her presence. I wanted to talk to her. Not just talk to her, but open myself up to her. The second thing I noticed about June was how tremendously overweight she was. She could not have been more than five feet tall and must have weighed well over two hundred pounds. I remember being surprised that I hadn't noticed her unusual size the moment I met her. She had short black hair, wore a bright red dress with lots of jewelry and appeared to be in her early fifties.

When we started talking, she went through my application with a fine-tooth comb. She asked me why I left Los Angeles for Santa Cruz and why I had chosen that particular university. She wanted to know why I picked the majors I had selected. She asked me quite a bit about why I had initially wanted to be a psychologist and how I had become interested in philosophy and gerontology. She asked me to tell her about my favorite teachers. She asked me about the sports I had played in college and high school and why I enjoyed them. I noticed the real delight she seemed to take in my successes in athletics. She asked about my job at the treatment center for emotionally-disturbed children and the sales job that followed. She asked what I wanted to do with my career and why. She was incredibly thorough. We spent quite a bit of time on each question. Moreover, I could tell that she was genuinely interested in my answers.

Throughout her questioning, my attention kept coming back to her eyes that at times had a childlike look of curiosity and acceptance. Then I'd look at her again and feel as though she were judging and interrogating me with a depth of perception I had never before experienced. She was both compelling and intimidating.

Regardless of the intimidating moments, I felt I had nailed the interview. I was surprised and happy at how well my answers had seemed to flow. I was very clear about how much I cared about people and how important it was for me to help them. I gave her examples from my days in gerontology (that always impressed people). I went into detail about all I had learned in my psychology classes. I explained how I took philosophy classes because they were difficult and I liked a challenge. I told her how difficult it had been working at the treatment center for such a low salary. I also added that it had been a good experience because I had the opportunity to help the kids, but I had figured out that industry was not for me. I told her how the last con artist company I worked for had failed to pay me my commissions. And I told her how much I cared about working for an honest person and, more than any other quality, I valued honesty above all else. I finished by telling her that I was an honest, caring person who really wanted to help others.

When I was through explaining myself she asked, "Would you like my thoughts?"

"Of course," I replied.

"You are the most dishonest person I think I have ever met."

June's comment went right to my core. I was shaken. My stomach suddenly turned upside down. I wanted desperately to defend myself, but my mouth wouldn't or couldn't move. So I just sat there while June went on. I felt like a live cadaver being dissected.

"You lie about everything. And what is worse, I don't think you know that you are even doing it. You say you wanted to study psychology so that you could help other people. But the truth is you took it so that you could understand yourself and impress other people. You said that you studied philosophy because it was a challenge. But you really took it because you liked the teacher. You said you got into gerontology because you like helping people. And I believe that you do like helping people. But that's not what really motivated you. You know it and I know it. You did the same thing with your job at the treatment center. You tell yourself you are helping other people, but the truth is you want other people to be impressed by you. You want to impress them because you're not impressed with yourself. You don't even like yourself. You lie to yourself, and then you actually believe the lie. Listen, you are a smart guy and I can see that you want to grow, but I honestly don't think I've ever met anyone who lies to themselves as much as you do. Let me ask you a question: with the exception of what you told me about graduating from school and what you did in sports, do you know that you are lying about just about everything else?"

I just sat there looking at her. I didn't know what to say. I felt like I had been abducted by aliens, and I was now on the mother ship. This was a strange place and nothing about it felt comfortable. From the moment I had selected my major in college, I had begun a process of honing my ability to cover up my fears and insecurities. After many years of practice, I had become a real professional. Everyone in my world was pretty good at covering up their insecurities. In fact, I had been covering up my weaknesses and fears for so long that I had forgotten that I was covering them up.

She was right. I was dishonest.

I had a story. No, I *was* a story. I was the guy who did what he did because he wanted to help other people. I was broke because I wanted to help others. I was out of work because I wanted to help others. I chose my majors because I cared about other people. Everyone liked my story. Some people even loved my story. Not this woman. Somehow this short, overweight, feisty woman knew what I had so conveniently forgotten – that I was a fraud. I was not being honest with myself or others. How ridiculous I must have appeared ending my high-powered interview presentation by telling her how much I valued honesty. Sitting across from her I suddenly became fully aware of what a false person I had become. My stomach was really hurting.

Then I had a flashback. As a boy I had made up an elaborate lie about owning a famous police dog. I told all the boys in my class about my famous dog and how he was able to help the police solve crimes. Many of the boys were interested, but one of my classmates took a particular interest in my pet. He was so impressed that he invited me over to his house and proceeded to tell his parents about my dog. His parents told my parents. The next thing I knew my parents wanted to have a talk with me about lying. Like most talented young liars, when confronted about my famous police dog, I decided to up the stakes and try to tell an even bigger lie. I explained to my parents that I did have a police dog, but they didn't know about him. Seeing that approach was making my parents even more upset, I was faced with no other alternative than to admit the truth. The funny thing was that it wasn't so awful. I had anticipated that getting caught would be this big terrible reality, but it wasn't bad at all. They talked to me. A finger was pointed in my face with a stern warning about the dangers of lying. Then it was over. I had been treated much worse for not cleaning up my room.

Sitting there in June's office, I realized that I was in a similar position. A sort of strange calm came over me. I said, "You're right. I do lie, but most of the time I honestly don't know that I'm doing it."

"Well, now we are getting somewhere. I think that was the first truly honest thing you've said in this interview."

In a subject shift that didn't seem that strange in this strange interview, June began to tell me about herself. She grew up in Boston, born one of eight children to a strict, first-generation Sicilian father and a loving, nurturing mother. The family belonged to an extremely legalistic Christian denomination. She grew up being told that wearing lipstick would send a young woman into hell. Her father beat any of the children who were caught breaking the rules, while her mother tried to protect them from their father's wrath.

As a teenager she discovered that she loved to sing. She would sing to anyone who would listen. It took a great deal of courage when, at age sixteen, she started sneaking out of her house (with the help of one of her sisters) to go to auditions. To make things even worse, these auditions were for opportunities to sing at the local mob-owned nightclubs. Even though she was self-taught and underage, June began getting singing gigs. She would sneak out at night while her father slept; knowing that if he ever caught her, she would be severely beaten. As her singing career began to blossom, her mother began to help her. Soon she was able to move out of her home and pursue her singing career in earnest. Eventually she sang with some of the bands that became famous in the Big Band era. She married George Gregory, a talented pianist. She loved him very much, but because of his ongoing infidelity, they divorced. She continued singing under her married name June Gregory.

At one point June decided to quit show business to tend to her dying mother. During the day she took care of her mom. At night she went to school to become a physician's assistant. After graduating, she went on to work for two extraordinary doctors. The first was a family practitioner and the second was a psychiatrist. Each doctor had taken her under his wing. They not only taught her about medicine, they also took a lot of time to teach her about diagnosing ailments. "They both had an uncanny ability to accurately diagnose their patients. It's more than just head knowledge. It really is an art," she said.

"After my mother passed away," June continued, "I couldn't handle being around sick people anymore. I left the medical field and decided to open a restaurant – June's Italian Villa. While I was waiting for the building permits to come through, I worked as a waitress at several other Italian restaurants. I studied everything they did. I wanted to be certain to learn everything: their mistakes and their successes. My restaurant turned out to be a tremendous success.

"Eventually I had to close the restaurant. I discovered that my bookkeeper had been embezzling from me. The guy's name was Ernie and, unfortunately, I had really grown to trust him. Looking back on it, I think he was jealous of my success. After that I worked in property management and then got into this business. Within one year, I became the top biller at the first agency I worked for. Then they started playing games with my commissions – saying one thing and doing another – so I left. The second agency was even worse; they were cutthroat. When I brought in a new client they would act excited and ask me all the details. I was still naïve, so I would tell them. Then they would turn right around and steal the account.

"A couple of the recruiters I respected decided to leave that agency and start their own, so I joined them. Unfortunately, one of them had some personal problems and had to leave. Now it's Ginger Leigh, Mary our receptionist, and me. Lately Ginger has been working from home. She's been very sick. Anyway, that's how we got the name of the agency, Gregory and Leigh."

Then she said, "You are probably wondering how I got so heavy. Would you like to know?"

I nodded. I was genuinely interested in hearing about June's life. She was so confident. She seemed to know, with absolutely certainty, that anything she did would be successful. She not only completely believed what she was saying; she had the track record to back it up. She was a force of nature and wasn't shy about it. I genuinely believed that she could do *anything* she set her mind to. There was an odd sense of vulnerability about her, but at the same time she was fearless.

June went on to explain that because she had grown up with such a strict and abusive father, she had picked the wrong kind of men to marry. Her religious background had convinced her that if she so much as kissed a guy, then she should marry him. She had been married and divorced three times. She had three daughters, one by each husband. She told me a little about each daughter. I could see that she loved them deeply. Because of her career in show business, men had always pursued her. A mother of three and deeply embarrassed by her three divorces, she unconsciously put on weight to keep men away. "It's stupid I know, but that's what happened," she said.

She told me her strengths and weaknesses so effortlessly, unashamed to admit her mistakes. In fact, she was *so* open and honest about her mistakes that somehow they didn't even sound like problems. Both her successes and her mistakes sounded equally interesting. It seemed to me that she wasn't covering up anything about herself. She was honest and real.

"The key to managing your career is to be honest with yourself," she said. "You don't have to be honest with anyone else, but your career will ride on your ability to be honest with yourself."

Even though I was overwhelmed and felt more than a little intimidated, I knew then that I wanted to work for her.

It's a Gut Feeling

Maggie was finishing her answer to Mark's question as my mind came back to the present time. She explained to him how she had known right away that she wanted to work for me. "I felt it in my gut. I just knew that it was the right place for me," she said.

"That's helpful," he said. Then he turned his attention back to me. "How would you answer the question?"

"You're right, based on a couple of interviews, if you're not completely committed to finding *exceptional* leadership as your first priority, it is impossible to determine their level of integrity and capability. On the other hand, if you are absolutely committed to the priority of wanting exceptional leadership, you will be shocked at just how easy it is to judge it correctly. You can do it based on a single interview. It's really the most natural thing in the world. I'm telling you, Mark, you would be surprised how good you would be at picking up on the level of integrity, honesty and business skills when those are the *only* things you are focused on."

"I guess so." Mark still sounded unconvinced.

I tried again. "What I'm talking about is using your intuitive mind rather than your analytical mind. The reason you have a problem understanding what I'm describing is that, up until this point, you have relied solely on your analytical mind to make decisions. You have an idea of what will make you happy in your career. You described it as a position with a venture capital firm, a start-up or a social networking internet firm. So you go out to a venture capital firm and they tell you about a position that matches what you want. They offer a salary you are happy with, and they throw in some promises of growth. They seem nice enough and, bingo, you have just found your ideal job. Hurray!"

"I must be missing something because, yes, that does sound good," he said. Now he was completely perplexed.

"There is only one problem. You didn't pay attention to how you felt about the integrity of the people you just met. And you dismissed the fact that, other than the few people you interviewed with, the people working at the company didn't appear to be very happy. In fact, when you look back on it, they looked hassled and stressed out. But those perceptions didn't matter to you because, after all, it was a venture capital firm and it was exactly the position you wanted. Are you getting the picture?"

"How do you know that I wouldn't pay attention to how the other people felt about working at the company?"

"History has a way of repeating itself in these circumstances. Even for a bright person like yourself."

"I don't understand," Mark said.

"It didn't even register on your radar how unhappy the people at your last company were until you started working there. My guess is you didn't figure it out until you had been there about, oh, two months."

"Yeah, that's about right," he said, laughing. "That's what you mean by using my analytical mind rather than my intuition?"

"Yes, your analytical mind says, 'Hey, Mark, this is exactly the job you are looking for. Go for it!' Meanwhile somewhere in your body, your gut is screaming, 'Something is not right here. These people don't look too happy. Warning! Warning!' Most people make decisions by choosing to listen only to their analytical mind. They ignore their gut feelings. It's a matter of perception. Your analytical mind perceives the interview from one perspective, your intuition from another. It depends on what priorities you choose to focus on in your job search and which of your perceptions you choose to pay attention to."

"Can you explain that a bit further?"

"Let's say a man named Joe is very focused on making a certain amount of money. Joe's first priority is to find a job that will pay him the amount he desires. He goes to an interview and discovers that the position not only pays the salary he wants, but it will actually pay him more. Immediately Joe's analytical mind says, 'Yes, this is it. This is great! This is exactly what I have been looking for.' Because the position meets what Joe desires most, his perception is that the position will meet all his needs and desires. That's where Joe and many others make their mistake.

And it's a very costly one. The analytical mind, having become so focused on money, makes an association between money and fulfillment. If left unchecked, the association will eventually become so strong that it will completely block out the intuitive mind's ability to weigh in on the situation. In hundreds of people I've interviewed, if the money is high enough, the person will perceive the environment as being good enough *no matter how bad it actually is*," I explained.

"I see what you're getting at. That's a really important point for me to remember. I feel like I should be writing this down."

"I think you'll remember it. Just keep in mind that we all struggle with these false associations."

"What's that?"

"A false association is when we link up a cause and an effect that have nothing to do with one another. For example, we believe a company that produces a product that impresses us will have leadership that we admire. Yet there is no connection between innovation and integrity. We believe a company that is very profitable must have good leadership. But many very profitable companies have been led by unethical and corrupt leaders. We believe a company that is willing to pay us the money we want must have leadership that is fair. Yet many companies pay higher salaries so their employees will put up with their unfair management practices. We believe a company that gives us the title or responsibilities of our dreams must know what it is doing. Yet, I don't know of any connection between getting the title and job you want and getting the respect and leadership you deserve."

"Yeah, you're right. I hadn't looked at it like that. So you're saying I shouldn't even be looking for a venture capital firm or a start-up?"

"Yes, that's exactly what I'm saying."

"Man, that's going to be tough. I really see myself working at a high-growth company."

"You have to keep in mind the first question I asked you after you described to me your ideal job. I'll ask you again: what if you find a high-growth company but discover you don't respect their leadership?"

"I don't know why that is so hard to hang on to. It's really such a simple point," Mark said, looking frustrated.

"Most people I counsel can grasp the idea that they want to work for people they respect. That part of the equation is easy. What separates the men from the boys are those who can let go of their images of success. You have to let go of your false associations if you are to have any chance at finding the quality of leadership I've been describing. Exceptional leadership is an incredibly rare and difficult find. You'll never find it if your focus and resolve is not absolute."

"It sounds like there is not much room for error."

"I cannot stress this point to you strongly enough. If you can't find the fortitude to let go of your false associations, then you will fall right back into the Matrix. The scary part is you won't even realize you are there."

"Can't I have both? Can't I find a venture capital firm or start-up that also has great leadership?"

"No, you can't."

"I don't understand. You're saying that there aren't any venture capital firms or start-ups that have good leadership?"

"You're not listening. I told you that you will not find a venture capital firm or a start-up with good leadership as long as you can't let go of the idea that you need it to be a venture capital firm or a start-up. If you keep insisting that your deepest needs and desires be met in the manner *you want them to be met*, then, yes, I'm saying you will never find what you are truly looking for."

Mark sat for a moment while neither one of us spoke. I looked over at Maggie again to see if she had anything to offer. She met my gaze with a blank stare. Finally, Mark spoke.

"I have to admit, this interview is not like anything I expected. But I really do appreciate what you're saying. No one has talked to me like this. To be honest, part of me really wants to disagree with you and argue the point. Believe me, when I want to put up an argument, I can be a real pain. But there is another part of me that, for some reason, feels relieved.

I don't understand why, but what you're telling me is taking the pressure off of me. It's like you're talking to me about things that I already knew but have for some reason forgotten."

"That's right," I said.

"I don't know why, but suddenly the idea of not working for a venture capital firm or start-up feels pretty good. In a strange way, it actually feels good to let go of the idea. The more I think about it, the more I think I can keep an open mind."

"The reason it's beginning to feel good is really very simple. As you let go of your false associations, you start to free yourself from your fears and reconnect with your true desires.

"I'm not sure I completely understand, but I would like to know how I can hang on to this."

"You have to know what your temptations are – what romances you away from making good choices. Otherwise, you will be vulnerable to being crushed by your false associations. For example, you would have as difficult a time discerning the quality of leadership of a fast-paced start-up as you would determining the character of a woman who is the exact physical type you are most attracted to."

Mark laughed. "Yeah, I can see that. Man, this is going to be tough for me to do!"

"Let me tell you a story about a false association I dealt with. It's not work related, but I think it will help you to remember the point."

"Please, go ahead."

"When I was a kid, about 10 or so, my dad took me camping at Mount Whitney, the tallest mountain in California. It was a really difficult climb for me. About halfway up the mountain, we stopped at a lake and set up camp for the night. We hadn't eaten all day. I was starving. My dad took out some fishing poles, and we caught several good-sized rainbow trout. My dad taught me how to clean the fish, and we got them ready to place over the campfire he had built. That trout was the best food I had ever tasted. It was a beautiful night. The sky was filled with stars. We stayed up late, and he told me stories while I watched as falling stars shoot across the sky. It was absolutely wonderful."

"That does sound great," Mark said.

"So, for the next 30 years, every time I went out to a nice restaurant I ordered trout. The problem is it never tasted very good. I always ended up coveting everyone else's food. As I was celebrating my 40th birthday at an especially nice restaurant, I was eating my trout and it suddenly hit me: *I don't like trout! I like camping with my dad.*"

"That must have been quite a revelation."

"Believe me, it was. My brain was suddenly filled with pictures of the hundreds of meals I had wasted ordering stupid trout. It also hit me how many times I had passed up opportunities to go camping with family and close friends, hundreds of great meals, fun times spent outdoors with relatives and friends. None of it ever happened because of one simple false association."

"It's funny that we are talking about this," Mark responded. "I could never put my finger on it until I was just listening to you, but I think I've had the feeling ever since graduating from college that I don't really know what I'm doing or where I'm going in my career. To be honest, I've been kind of afraid that there is something wrong with me. So many of my friends seem to know exactly what they want to be. I feel like I should know. I have to admit, I've gotten good at hiding my fear and confusion from other people. Everyone sees me as this focused, ambitious guy. But I think a lot of that is just my way of covering up the fact that I'm not really sure what I want to do."

As I looked at Mark, I saw that he was no longer the same guy I had been talking with 20 minutes earlier. Having made the decision to let go of his false associations, the fear that had been driving him had been exposed. False associations always cover up some great fear. Once the fear is exposed and overcome, the individual is freer to connect to his desires. This new-found freedom results in a marked improvement in the ability to discern and attract a job that meets deeper needs, dreams and passions. Instead of being hyper and intense, Mark was now calm and confident. He was slowly becoming more comfortable being himself. I had a fleeting thought that June would have really liked this guy.

I continued, "Those people you're talking about don't know what they want to be any more than you do. Our careers are defined by relationships, not by accomplishments. We are relational to the core. When it comes to really knowing what we want in our careers, the only thing we know for certain is WHO, not WHAT, we would like to become as a person. We all have a sense of our potential as individuals. We make strides toward that potential or away from it primarily through the people with whom we choose to surround ourselves, especially those we choose as our leaders. The certainty you saw in those other people is mostly based on false associations."

Mark was tracking with me. "That's interesting. I never looked at it like that. I guess, in a sense, the fact that I've never really been sure what I wanted to do is a good thing. Wow, that changes things, doesn't it? I've always wondered why people who are so sure of what they want to do can never give me a compelling reason why they want to do it or, if they are already in their careers, why they seem to have less passion for it as time goes by. It seems to me that if you are doing what you truly love, you would enjoy it more the longer you do it."

"When it's on target, you do enjoy it more the longer you do it," I said.

Mark had another observation. "The other thing I noticed is that other people could never help me figure out what I wanted to do. It was like they had arrived at what they wanted through some mysterious formula that worked for them but didn't apply to me. When I look at it from your perspective, everything starts to make sense," he said.

"The big problem with the way we think about our careers is that from the very start, we have been trained to ask ourselves the wrong question. We ask ourselves: *What* do I want to be? If we could be totally honest with ourselves, I think we would all admit that the question makes us feel uncertain and insecure. Since there is no *what* (no title, no responsibility, no industry, etc.)

that will bring a person fulfillment and growth in and of itself, '*What* do I want to be?' can only lead a person down the wrong path."

"So what's the right question?" Mark asked.

"'Who do I want to be?' is a much better question. Think about it a moment. If I told you that if you took this particular path in your career, you would end up experiencing the greatest amount of passion, fulfillment, growth and meaningful accomplishment possible, would you have any reason to care what your responsibilities and duties were? If I told you that if you followed me, I could lead you to a career that would bring out the very best in you, would it matter to you what industry it was in? If I told you that you could experience more confidence than you ever felt before, would you argue over your title? If I told you that if you listen to what I'm telling you, you will discover more inner strength and purpose than you ever thought possible, would you need to negotiate over salary or care what others' opinions of you were? All this begins to come into focus when you ask yourself the question '*Who* do I want to be?' instead of '*What* do I want to do?'"

"That's still a little vague. Can you explain it again to me?" Mark asked.

"Your ultimate career dream is to become the best person you can possibly become. That's the deepest desire in your career and mine. Most of us, when it comes down to it, share that same dream. This is true whether you are aware of it or not. It's true even for those determined individuals who will look you in the eyes and swear to you that it doesn't apply to them. It's the dream that's been written into our souls since the day we were born. Many, perhaps most, have given up on that dream. But I assure you that no matter how deeply buried beneath the surface it may be, it's there in us. Since the ultimate desire in our career is to become *who* we are capable of becoming, the question '*Who* do I want to be?' better directs us toward our deeper goals and aspirations. The question gets at the heart of what we really want most and leads us away from a career based on false associations."

"Okay, once I get a picture of who I want to become, then what?"

"Good question. Do you have that picture?"

"Yes, I think I do. I have this image of myself as totally successful. Not successful in the sense that I just have a lot of money or that other people think highly of me, although I wouldn't mind that. But I see myself being really proud of myself, having a lot of integrity and making a real difference in the lives of others. I also see myself working on or having accomplished something that means a lot to me. I guess that's it." Mark was "in the zone" now.

"That's a good answer," I affirmed. "You must have given it some thought before today."

I had the thought, if Mark only knew how much further along he was than I was at his age, he would really appreciate what I was trying to tell him. I was doing my best to teach him what June had taught me. I then remembered something the great theologian Oswald Chambers once said, "You can never give another person that which you found, but you can make them homesick for what you have." I was trying to make Mark homesick, just as June had done for me.

"Yes, I've had this picture of myself for some time now," Mark said. "I just didn't know that it was that important. Or maybe I didn't think it was possible. I don't know."

"I'm glad you can see yourself that way. It gives you something to shoot for, doesn't it?"

"Yes, it does. You know I just realized that I have the exact opposite feeling than I had when I walked in here today. I felt that I needed a job, and it really didn't matter what job I got as long as it fit my expectations. But my expectations were so low compared to how I see myself now. I would have totally compromised myself."

"That is why the question '*Who* do I want to be?' is so important. You see yourself as a man with a lot of integrity, accomplishing something that you are proud of, something that makes a difference in the lives of others. Given everything you have learned here today, tell me the best and fastest way to achieve that dream."

Mark hesitated a moment, then I saw the light turn on. "To work for someone who has those qualities."

"That's right. It's remarkably simple when you get right down to it. The key to becoming the person you dream of becoming is to work for leaders who have the qualities you admire and want to develop."

"You keep saying 'leadership,' but can't it be accomplished working for a manager in a company as well?"

"No, it can't. The essential relationship is with the leadership. If you work for a great manager with all the qualities you admire within a company where the leadership lacks those qualities, you will soon discover one of two things: either your manager will leave the company once he or she discovers the truth about the leadership or your manager is a person who may believe in all the same values you aspire to but, unlike you, he or she is not willing to act on those convictions. Because of that lack of courage, you will soon lose as much respect for the manager as you have lost for the leadership of the company."

"Is that always the case?"

"No, there are some exceptions. There are individuals who choose to stay in compromised work situations because their work is a means to an end toward a greater purpose. That purpose brings them the same level of passion, fulfillment and growth a healthier environment with a better leader would bring them. But I must tell you those situations are becoming increasingly rare. The true litmus test is the overall sense of fulfillment and pride that people take in their work. If it's high then they have chosen the negatives of their job honestly and with integrity. If they are not happy, they are lying to themselves, playing the martyr."

"I'm not quite sure about what you mean by 'chosen the negatives.'"

"In every work opportunity, there are going to be negatives. Even the very best leaders have negatives. What makes for a great work relationship is not that there aren't negatives, but the negatives have been discussed openly and both sides choose to go forward in spite of them. That's the reason why focusing on integrity is so crucial to your career growth. Without integrity in leadership, you don't have the opportunity to choose the negatives because you haven't been told what they are. Nothing will take the wind out of your sails faster in a job than discovering that you have been lied to by the leadership. Betrayal kills relationships."

"What if the leadership does have integrity, but you just can't deal with the negatives they are telling you about in the interview?"

"You have hit upon the key to good decision making. You have to be honest with yourself. My boss June used to say, 'The single most important key to career growth is the ability to be honest with yourself.' She would add it didn't even matter if you lied to everyone else as long as you were honest with yourself. She told me I would know people of integrity by their ability to be honest about their negatives. 'Anyone can be honest about their pluses; it takes courage and self-awareness to be honest about the negatives.'

"Once you know the leadership's negatives and they know yours, you are free to choose. If it's a negative you don't want to deal with or simply can't handle, then move on. But you must realize that the most common negative you will find in your career is the one we have been talking about today – a lack of integrity in leadership. So don't be too quick to dismiss an opportunity where there is integrity. As I mentioned, they are very rare."

"I guess its true most people never get to work in the kind of relationship you are describing?" Mark asked.

"If they have experienced it, it usually occurred at the beginning of their work life, in their first or second job before they can build up a lot of false associations. They are still operating on intuition. They take a job because the people seemed 'pretty cool.' And it turns out the job is pretty cool. Later they have a long list of things they are looking for, all false associations, and 'pretty cool' isn't in the top five. In fact, it's not even in the top ten."

"That's kind of sad, don't you think?"

"Yes, it's very sad. That's why the talk we are having is so important to how you think about your future. The Native Americans used to have a method of hunting buffalo that reminds me of the way we, as a culture, are managing our careers. They would run the herd into a stampede – a panic mode – and then direct them to a nearby cliff where the herd would fall to its death. Hunt over. That's how I see a lot of people's careers.

"What do you mean?"

"Many are running fast toward better money, titles, industries, education, retirement, financial independence, survival – you name it. Unfortunately, what they are running toward has nothing to do with their well being. The more they run toward things that aren't bringing them fulfillment, the quicker they find themselves in a panic mode and the harder they run. For far too many people, the work world has become a stampede and, without knowing it, they are headed right toward a cliff. And, for those who don't identify and let go of their false associations, they become addictions."

"Addictions, isn't that a rather strong term?" Mark asked.

"That's exactly what they become. We all know people who have made a lot of money but are obsessed with making more. Perhaps, when they began their career, making money brought them a lot of satisfaction and validation. Unknowingly, they formed a false association between money and their need and desire for validation, meaningful accomplishment, integrity and fulfillment. That false association creates a psychological reality where their needs and desires are not being met. The longer those needs and desires go unmet, the greater they become. The greater they become, the more that person looks to making more money to fulfill them. The more they make, the more they need it. That's the vicious circle of unmet desire. Money, for this person, is no longer a source of validation and satisfaction. It becomes an insatiable need. That's an addiction to money. It's no different than an addiction to drugs. It just looks more respectable. Or consider people who have successfully climbed the ladder of success, but feel that they are never quite high enough. That's an addiction to status or to what other people think of them. The mother who obsesses about her child's health or well-being is addicted to her role as a caregiver. I'm describing situations where the person's identity has become falsely associated with *what* they do rather than *who* they truly are. The false association has disconnected them from their actual needs and desires."

Mark nodded with understanding. "I can see how that is true of a lot of the people I know."

"If you want to avoid these career addictions, then you are going to have to work hard to stop following the herd. And if you do choose to go against the herd, you are going to be hit by a lot of buffalo who are mad at you for going the 'wrong' way. It's very easy to fall back into thinking you are going the wrong direction, especially when you are going up against a stampede."

Thoughtfully Mark said, "I suppose some of the buffalo that I'm going to hit are going to be my friends and family?"

"Yes, that's almost always the first true test of your career. In many ways, it's also the most difficult. Your family and friends want the best for you. Unfortunately, their perspectives are often mired in their own false associations. You have to accept the spirit in which they offer their advice but not compromise yourself when they get upset with you for not following it," I said.

"How will I know when I find the right opportunity?"

"Actually, it will be very simple. Bring to the interview the Mark you described to me earlier – the one who is confident – the Mark who knows who he wants to be. See yourself as that guy. I mean really experience what it would feel like to be him. If after interviewing with the company, that Mark feels passionately alive, chances are you have found the right position."

"You're saying that the guy I want to be will be put asleep by the wrong environment?"

"Let's just say if you do what I just described, you will know if the situation is right for you."

"Intuitively?"

"Yes, you'll be amazed."

"That's interesting. I want you to know I believe I can do this. I've always had a sense that I wasn't going to do what other people expected of me. I just want to feel like I do right now: like I can just be myself and at the same time grow toward becoming my best self. Does that make sense?" Mark asked.

"Yes, it makes all the sense in the world. If you want it, you're going to have to do two things: first, you must make your dream clear by focusing on that person you see yourself becoming. Secondly, you have to let go of all your false associations of how you see your success happening. You have to let go of every expectation you have associated with your success."

"I know that you have mentioned some of them, but what would you say are the major false associations people get stuck on?"

"I was just reading a book called *Emotionally Healthy Spirituality* by Peter Scazzero." I looked around my desk and found the book. "Here's how this author described the top three false associations: 1) You are what you do. 2) You are what you have. 3) You are what other people think of you."

"If I'm not any of those things, then what am I?"

"That's a very good question. If you can answer it you will have discovered what you desire most in your career. You will have found your dream: to be your true and best self. That is your new job. You came in here today wanting a new opportunity, well, now you have one. What you want most in your career is not something you will find out in the job market. It's something you can choose to live from at any moment, no matter what circumstances you currently find yourself in. I'm not saying this is easy. Dealing with unexpected adversity, rejection and job loss is incredibly challenging and, at best, takes time to sort out. But the great reality of your career is you can have what you want most at any moment in time. I'm living my career dream right now talking with you, Mark."

"Yes, that's it. That's what I've always wanted. I've been looking for it frantically everywhere: in school, in the careers of other people, in the job market and it's been right here all the time."

"Here's how serious the problem of false associations is in our world. Several years ago a survey was taken among college students. They were asked if they could choose any career, what would be their first choice. The number one choice that year was to become an attorney. That same year another survey was taken among people in the workplace. This survey was measuring fulfillment. Guess what profession was voted dead last?"

"Attorneys?"

"You got it. That year they replaced dentists as the career people found to be most stressful and *least* fulfilling."

"That's what you mean by 'buffalo off the cliff.'"

"Yes, this is very real. In the vision you had of yourself, you weren't focused on what you did, how much you made or what other people thought of you. It's not that those things didn't matter, but they were not primary. You said you wanted to be proud of the person you had become. That's not the same as believing that you are what you do. You said that you wanted to accomplish something that makes a difference in the lives of others. That's not the same as believing that your self-worth is measured by your material worth. You said that you wanted to have your integrity intact. That's not the same as being motivated by status or what other people think of you."

"You're right. It's so difficult to hang on to that vision. I have it one minute then I lose it the next."

"You're not alone. That's true of all of us."

"So how do I hang on to it?" Mark asked.

"You know the answer to that."

"It just all keeps coming back to who I choose as my leader? It's really that simple?"

"You tell me. Do you think avoiding all your false associations and getting singularly focused on finding a leader who has the qualities you described in your vision is simple?"

"No, it's not going to be easy. But I believe I can do it, with your help that is."

"If you get committed, I'll help you."

"Given all these changes, how do I go about marketing myself?"

"You want to use everything you have in order to attract the best leadership you can find. The ideal job is one working for the quality of leadership you dream of, combined with using as many of your skills, attributes, experience and education as possible. Your background is what you have to offer the leadership you're looking for. The more marketable you are, the more companies you attract, the more likely it becomes that you will find exceptional leadership. Although I can tell you that I was the least marketable person I know of, and I found the most remarkable leader I have ever run across."

"That sounds like a very interesting story."

Thoughts of my time with June flooded my mind: How she had hired me even though I really had nothing to offer. How she had confronted me on all my negatives: my rage, my overwhelming fears and insecurities, my lack of common sense and business knowledge, how I dressed, how I treated others, my low self-image, my lack of self-honesty and my inability to give. Thoughts of all the laughs, adventures and countless victories came to me as well: our long talks, celebrations and, of course, all the placements we worked on together.

All that I had become, I owed to her mind-blowing wisdom, courage, generosity and involvement. I couldn't believe that she had been gone for four years. She was still so present.

I looked across the table at Mark. Something told me that we would be placing him soon.

"It is," I said, "it really is."

Brian

Every career story is full of good motivations and bad, good decisions and poor ones, victorious moments and ugly ones. To get the full appreciation of what June was up to in people's lives, I will tell you two stories: my story and the story of the candidates she worked with.

As you read, you will soon discover these two separate stories begin to meld into one. June's influence on the candidates inspired me to grow and, in turn, my growth motivated the candidates to seek out careers that brought out the best in them.

But I'm getting ahead of myself. Let's start at the beginning…

I wanted to be Spider-Man. I wanted to be Spider-Man so badly that it hurt! He was so cool. He was everything I could ever imagine becoming: He had super human powers. He could walk up the sides of buildings (very cool!). He helped save people but never wanted credit for it. And he had the best costume of any of the superheroes. Every cell in my four-year-old body was excited about the prospect of becoming Spider-Man. It was crystal clear to me that when I grew up and became Spider-Man, my life would be absolutely complete. Achieving this goal would bring me joy and fulfillment beyond my wildest dreams. Becoming Spider-Man meant absolute freedom, constant adventure and fun. Last but not least, being Spider-Man meant saving the world from certain destruction. (There are some really BAD guys out there!)

For passion and desire, there's nothing like your first dream.

After about three months of dreaming with all my young heart and soul of becoming Spider-Man, I woke up one morning and decided that I no longer wanted to be a superhero. I wanted to be a fireman. This was, in effect, my first career change. With all the same excitement, passion and determination that I had felt toward Spider-Man, becoming a fireman meant everything to me. Being a superhero was old news; becoming a fireman was the one and only true career for me.

So there I was, at age five, clear as I could be about my amazing career as a fireman, when something very strange and significant happened: School. I never saw it coming!

One day I was told that I was about to begin my new life: not as a fireman, but rather as a kindergartner. This news came as quite a shock. I wasn't even sure what kindergartners did. From what I was able to gather from adults, they spent most of their time doing something called "learning." All the grownups seemed very excited about this thing called learning. After someone explained to me what learning meant, I remember thinking I must have a lot to learn because I didn't find anything at all exciting about it. In fact, compared to being a fireman, learning seemed pretty dull.

Then another very important event happened in my career. I was told that in order to become a fireman, I had to go to school. *That's terrible news*, I remember thinking. First I find out I have to go to school instead of living my dream of becoming a fireman. Now I'm being told that I not only have to go to school, but I have to do well at it. *Why do I have to do well at something I don't want to do in order to do what I really want to do?* My five-year-old mind reasoned. Just to add fuel to the flames, the grownups were acting as though I was somehow supposed to be happy about all this. I had received the worst possible news about my future! What was wrong with these people?

Going to school was my first exposure to the real world. At age five, I was already beginning to understand that my dreams were not going to come true the way I hoped. Like most children, this was the first major setback in my young career. It is a disappointment many of us never recover from. The sad realization I would not be riding around in a fire truck anytime soon and that my days would be filled with learning was a tremendous disappointment. A disappointment I can clearly recall, I'm embarrassed to admit, some 40 years later.

The first thing I learned about school is that I didn't like it. I wouldn't have liked anything that stood between me and becoming a fireman. But I was especially outraged that I had to spend so much time at it. It only added to my frustration that no one was the least bit sympathetic about my tremendous setback. My school career was off to a very bad start.

Somewhere as a young boy or girl, your career took this same turn. I hope and pray your transition went much better than mine. I hope you were excited about the prospect of going to school. I hope you were as excited knowing you were going to school as I would have been to become a fireman. But whether you found the news about your new career as a student to be positive or disappointing, one thing is true: we did not have an option.

The first lesson of my school experience was: you must do well at something other than what you dream of in order for that dream to come true. I accepted this early disappointment as a fundamental reality. Anyone whose favorite class was recess knows exactly what I'm talking about.

As motivation I was told if I did well at elementary school, I would get what I wanted when I got older. However, about three weeks into my kindergarten career, I no longer dreamed of being a fireman. I didn't have the time or inclination to think about my dream. All I wanted was to learn to read the first word in my Blue Book Reader. (The Blue Book was for the slow learners and the first word was "The").

Attending school made me aware of a sad and humiliating limitation. I hadn't yet learned how to talk. Let me explain.

My grandmother had suffered from mental illness. She had many strange rules for her daughter, my future mom. One of those rules was that her daughter could not leave the house for any reason except to go to school. The threat of punishment for breaking this rule was diabolical. Every day my mom obeyed until the night of her senior prom. That night she decided to take a chance and sneak out of the house.

When she returned home she could not find her mother. She looked everywhere and finally out of desperation looked inside a broom closet. There she found her mother's dead body hanging by a rope. The threat fulfilled.

My mom never recovered. Even worse, she was left alone with an abusive father. To escape, she married my dad when she was 18 and gave birth to me a year later. Deeply wounded and full of rage, she was not equipped to be a mother. Struggling with her own difficulties, she was so unfocused that she would often take me places and forget to take me home with her when she left. I found myself alone and frightened in stores, restaurants and a variety of other places. By age five, the emotional and physical abuse I had gone through had stunted my verbal development. My mom could understand me, but when I went to school I learned no one else could. Rather than going through the constant stress and humiliation of not being understood, I decided to stop talking altogether. From the time I started school, I rarely – if ever – uttered a word.

Like everyone else my age, I went to school five days a week for nine months out of the year. Unfortunately, I spent a great deal of my time daydreaming and looking forward to just about anything that didn't have to do with school itself. I never learned how to enjoy learning and as a result, I wasn't very good at it. I failed all the way through the second grade. At that point I was placed in a special after-school program to learn how to talk and eventually read. The program was excellent. Within a few years, I was beginning to communicate well enough so others could understand me. I was also beginning to read and write. Unfortunately, given my poor start I was still the worst student in school. Because of the humiliation I had associated with my inability to learn how to speak or read, I still hated school. Learning itself made me very uncomfortable. Life continued like this for three more long years. Then one day everything changed.

Her name was Mrs. Brown. She was my fifth grade teacher. I think almost everyone has had a Mrs. Brown in their school career. Mrs. Brown loved to teach. She was funny, smart and caring. She wore beautiful dresses and had a warm, wonderful smile. Mrs. Brown took a genuine interest in each of her students, and I was no exception. I basked in her attention. I wanted to do a good job for her. I wanted to talk more clearly and read more often. Mrs. Brown came up with the idea of making paper maché dinosaurs. Wow! The entire class got into it. She was brilliant! She especially enjoyed teaching us to write and sing. I couldn't sing well, but I enjoyed the writing assignments. Ms. Brown gave me a lot of encouragement and praise for everything I turned in.

After a six-year hiatus from dreams, I had a new one: I wanted to be a writer. I wrote story after story. My 10-year-old passions were rekindled. My career was back on track.

The next year I had a teacher whose name I cannot remember, but she was no Mrs. Brown. In fact, it wouldn't be until college that I would experience another Mrs. Brown. As the years of school went by, I no longer dreamed of being a writer. I thought of being a basketball or baseball player, but those careers didn't have the same positive impact on me as my earlier dreams.

Then I came upon the new game in town: getting into college. If I didn't do well in middle school, I was told in no uncertain terms, I wouldn't be able to do what I wanted (whatever that was) when I got older. Everything I did in school "counted." Grades "counted." Attitude "counted." Number of sick days "counted." The kind of classes I took "counted." One failed class could affect my entire future. Not getting into a good college meant I probably wouldn't be happy as an adult. Not getting into a good college meant not making a good living. Not getting into college, I was led to believe, meant being relegated to being a second-class human being for the rest of my life.

Given all that I understood to be on the line, I felt a great deal of pressure to do well in school. I didn't know what I wanted to become, I didn't have a dream, but I knew I didn't want to be a failure. So doing well in school became my goal. Not failing became my target. I spent many sleepless nights worrying about my grades. The worrying paid off; I got through high school with good enough grades and SAT scores to go to a good college.

On the down side, I had also become extremely good at worrying.

I picked the University of California at Santa Cruz for two reasons. The first and most important was I wanted to get as far away from my family as possible. My parents divorced when I was 14. My dad offered to take me with him. He promised to make up for all the time he had missed being a good dad. He confessed to me he had been in a series of affairs throughout the marriage and wanted to make it up to me. (Note to dads, please don't confess having affairs to your young son. Trust me, he doesn't want to know). Meanwhile, life with my mom was becoming increasingly unbearable. I was becoming physically strong enough to fight back against her abuse. In one episode in which I was trying to defend myself, I ended up pinning her down. It was an awful situation. On the one hand, I didn't want to let her up for fear that she would hurt me. On the other hand, I didn't want to keep her pinned down for fear that I might hurt her. My dad's invitation was just the miracle I was looking for. I was not only getting away from my mom's abuse, I was getting my dad back.

Unfortunately, the fairy tale didn't last very long. After three months of living with my dad, he was as absent as ever. Then he came home late one night to announce we were moving in with a woman he had just met. She had four children of her own. The next thing I knew he was telling me we were all now a family. But the reality was my dad's attentions were turned toward winning over the affections of her children. I found myself reeling, completely betrayed.

I had believed in my dad. When I tried to talk to him about how I felt, he told me that he was actually doing the whole thing for me. It's one thing to be betrayed by your father; it's another for him to try and convince you it's for your own good. But he was my dad, so I tried to believe him. With no one to talk to, my pain quickly turned to rage. I was mean to my future stepmother, and I bullied her four children.

My second reason for choosing the school I did was far less complicated. The campus was perched on the edge of a beautiful forest on a hillside overlooking Monterey Bay. Those were my reasons. I knew nothing else about the school. I had never been there. I knew nothing about its reputation other than the University of California system was supposed to have some of the best schools in the state.

With my fears of abandonment and betrayal deeply rooted in the core of my being, I arrived at the university feeling completely lost. I knew only one person and had no idea what I was doing or why I was doing it. On my first day, I met with an academic advisor.

This was the second significant experience of my young career. The advisor brought me into her office, smiled at me, and asked me the big question, "So, Brian, what do you want to major in? What do you want to do with your life?"

Every cell in my body heard the question. Not one of them had an answer.

I suppose if I could have answered her honestly, it would have gone something like this: "Listen, lady, I just got here, and I haven't the foggiest idea what I'm doing, let alone what I want to do with my life. But if you must know, I started out wanting to be Spider-Man. Then I wanted to be a fireman. My dreams got put off when I found out I had to attend school for the next thirteen years, which is an extremely long time when you're only five. Anyway, I didn't do so well at school at first but then I met a great teacher named Mrs. Brown. She made me feel real good about myself and my ability to write. So I thought that I wanted to be a writer. But then fifth grade ended and Mrs. Brown was no longer my teacher. I don't remember the names of any of my next teachers because they weren't very good, which means school got really boring again. At that point I lost all interest in becoming anything at all, until I found out that everything counted. I was informed that if I didn't do well in middle school and high school I couldn't become what I wanted when I grew up. I became so afraid of being a loser I got motivated to do well in school. Oh, by the way, did I mention I haven't seen or heard from my crazy mom in four years and that my dad sold me out for a woman with four kids? I picked a school in California to be as far from my wacked-out family as I could. I would have gone out of state, heck I would have gone out of this universe to get away from them. But the only schools I could afford are in this state. The only thing I know for certain is I want to be close to the ocean and mountains. I don't suppose I can major in 'I like the ocean and mountains.' So here I am. I know one person. I don't have much money. I haven't had a positive thought about myself, let alone my future, in as long as I can remember and you're asking me 'what do you want to do with the rest of your life?' Gee, lady, if you really need an answer I'm going to have to go with, "*I HAVE ABSOLUTELY NO FRICKIN' IDEA!*"

Instead I sheepishly asked, "What are my options?"

She handed me a list of majors. I could eliminate many of them right away. I knew I didn't want to do anything that involved a lot of math, so the sciences were out. Some of the majors that were listed I had never heard of. How can you major in a subject you've never heard of? Those were out. By this process of elimination, I was able to whittle the list down to about six or seven choices. I saw psychology and thought, because I couldn't figure myself out, it might be helpful to know how to figure out others.

And there it was. I was now a psychology major. My future decided, I asked the advisor if she could tell me how to get back to my dorm. The college was large, and I had no idea where I was.

Brian

Someone very wise once made the observation, "It takes people at least five years to recover from college." I was about to find out what they meant.

As I was about to embark on my college education, I knew intuitively that something was very wrong. I had just committed to becoming a psychologist, and I didn't really want to be one. The thought of becoming a psychologist didn't have any of the same excitement, passion or motivation of my earlier dreams of becoming Spider-Man, a fireman or a writer. I could have chosen to become an English major if I really wanted to become a writer, but the idea of taking a lot of English classes was unappealing. I'd rather throw the dice and try a subject I knew nothing about. Still, I was left with a very uncomfortable feeling I was somehow performing for other people. I chose psychologist not because I really wanted to be one, but because I wanted to impress others. Psychologists, I assumed, understand people.

If I could succeed in psychological counseling, maybe I could fool people into believing I wasn't some loser who had no idea of what I really wanted. In other words, if I could learn how other people's minds work, maybe I could get really good at covering up the fact that something was terribly wrong with mine. Why didn't I know what I wanted to be? I had decided to make a career out of covering up my insecurity. As a professional phony, I would help heal other people's neuroses. That was my career plan.

At the beginning of my second year in college, another wonderful career event took place. I had a great professor in my Greek philosophy class. Mr. Santiago was the male version of Mrs. Brown – my fifth grade teacher. He was extremely funny, had great passion for teaching and took a genuine interest in his students. Mr. Santiago used Greek philosophy as a back drop; his true mission was to teach us about life, real life. He taught us life should be adventurous. He taught us about the importance of keeping commitments and what it means to take responsibility for your actions. Having been through World War II, he told us stories about how difficult life could be and how to find meaning in overcoming our obstacles. He taught us the importance of not taking ourselves too seriously. He enjoyed life and tried with all his heart and soul to teach us what he had learned. He taught us by showing us how much fun learning can be when done by an exceptional teacher passionate about his craft. He did all this and, somewhere along the way, managed to teach us quite a bit about Greek philosophy.

His class was not easy. His tests were some of the most difficult I had ever taken. Because I liked the class so much, I poured myself into my mid-quarter paper. I thought it was the best thing I had ever written. When I got the paper back, I was shocked to find out that my grade was F. He said that it was very well-written, but he pointed out that one of the fundamental hypotheses of my argument was incorrect. All of my following assumptions, while well thought out, were just plain wrong.

I was dumbfounded. I hadn't received a failing grade on a paper since the fourth grade. But when I went back and reread what I had written, I saw he was right. I was so caught up in writing a great paper, it didn't occur to me to think the subject through. No other teacher had cared about the deeper issues. This may sound strange to you but, at the time, I liked that he gave me an F. Mr. Santiago, it hit me, really cared.

Inspired, I went down to the administrative office and asked to change my major to philosophy. I wanted to be like Mr. Santiago. If studying philosophy would help me get there, I was willing to do whatever it took. The counselor did not like the idea of me changing majors. After a long debate, we settled on a compromise. I would now have a double major in psychology and philosophy.

Mr. Santiago's class came to an end and, like my experience with Mrs. Brown, eventually so did my excitement and motivation. Almost as if to punish me for enjoying Mr. Santiago, my next professors were awful. My college experience returned to its previous uninspired state. And that's how it continued until my junior year when I took a night job at a local nursing home.

As a night shift orderly, my job was to attend to the residents' needs. My duties included changing the beds of patients who wet or soiled themselves, moving patients in their sleep to avoid bed sores, talking to residents who could not sleep, assisting patients to the restroom etc. My favorite part of the job was talking with the patients. Some of them had lived remarkable lives. There was the patient who had been one of the first women to graduate from the University of Chicago and had gone on to play professional golf. There was the man who had owned most of the farmland in Santa Cruz, land that was now worth a large fortune. There was the woman who was blind and very near death but who always managed to have a smile and a good word for me. There were also plenty of negative patients – screamers, complainers and people in so much pain that I couldn't help but wish that God would take them as soon as possible. (That must sound awful, but anyone who has worked in a nursing home understands thoughts like this go with the job.) Every night was an incredible adventure in seeing the very best and worst that life had to offer. Facing death, there were heroes and cowards and everything in between. And, sadly, over the year that I worked there, most of them died. As they passed away, I began to get a clear understanding that my life would end someday too. This sobering realization got me motivated to do something with my education. Like the residents I had grown to admire, I wanted to have a good story to tell at the end of my days.

With this newly-found motivation I began to study gerontology – the study of aging and old age. I wanted to do something positive for my new friends. I figured that the university had a lot of students and the nursing homes in the area had a lot of patients. Why not put the two together? I applied and received a grant that would pay all my expenses for a project I put together that would give university students college credit to spend time at any of the local nursing homes. The project was a success with the students, and the residents enjoyed and benefited from their newly formed relationships. As a result of the project, I was asked to teach an undergraduate class in gerontology. I felt I had really found my life's work. I read as much as I could in the emerging study of aging. It was clear to me I was going to become a gerontologist.

My personal life wasn't going quite as well. My girlfriend at the time informed me that she had received a scholarship to go to France to study mime. I was brokenhearted. As a parting gift she had the idea to set me up on a date with her roommate, Robin. The date didn't go well. I found it difficult to communicate with her or feel close to her. She had a lot of positive qualities, but it just wasn't a good match. That's what I knew to be true, but it's not what I acted on.

I didn't want to be alone, so I continued to see her. Then I found myself needing to see her. Before long, we were a couple. As was the Santa Cruz custom at the time, after dating for about six months we decided to move in together. I began to see Robin as being a better person than I was. She seemed to love me for all the right reasons. It occurred to me that if I could continue to be around her I might become a better person. I knew my reasons for continuing the relationship were primarily out of fear. I also knew I was finding myself very attracted to other women. At one point, I had a flirtation with a woman at work. When I told Robin about it, she was deeply hurt. Upset with myself for hurting her, afraid to be alone, scared that I might run out of money and have to hit the streets, I asked her if getting married would make her feel better. She cheered up and accepted.

A couple of weeks after making the decision to get married, we discovered that Robin was pregnant. I already felt like a complete impostor for getting married. Now I was to become a father. The thought of it scared me out of my mind. I knew I was the last guy on earth who was qualified to be a father. That day I went for a drive and had a very strong inclination to just keep going. I wanted to escape. But I made the decision I was going to return home to marry Robin and try to be the best dad I knew how to be. My career as a phony was taking on a much larger dimension than I had ever imagined.

Eight months later, my daughter Jessamyn was born. She was absolutely the most beautiful thing I had ever seen. The day of her birth, I sat down and wrote her a letter. I promised her I would try to do everything I could to work out my problems, so she could someday have the father she deserved, one she could admire. It was a promise that was a lot easier to write than to keep.

As I approached graduation, I researched the best graduate schools in gerontology. There was one stand-out program at Northwestern University in Chicago. I applied to the program knowing they accepted 3 students a year from an applicant pool of more than 300. Despite the odds, I was certain I would get in. My project had been a big success and had received attention by influential people in the field. Not only was I quite sure of my acceptance, I was also confident they would offer me a scholarship because I had no way of affording the program. Friends and advisors encouraged me to apply to other programs, but I was so sure that Northwestern was my destiny that I didn't take their advice.

Meanwhile, I had to pay the bills. Several of my fellow psychology students had gone to work at a residential treatment home for emotionally-disturbed teenagers. They claimed that the experience would be looked at very positively by graduate schools. Needing a break from my late night shifts at the nursing home, I applied and got the position as a group home counselor. I knew the position would be short-lived until I moved to Chicago.

After what seemed like an eternity, a letter arrived from Northwestern. I was one of nine students being invited to interview for one of the three spots. My instincts had been correct! A good friend loaned me the money to fly to Chicago for the interview. Since I already knew that I was going to be selected, I wasn't nervous during the panel interview. I did notice that one of the interviewers didn't seem to like me very much or perhaps, more accurately, didn't think much of the school I attended. At the end of the interview they thanked me for coming, and with a big smile the head professor proclaimed the interview had gone extremely well. Then he asked one of the graduate students to show me around the campus and the student housing. "I'm sure we will be seeing you again soon," he said.

My dream of becoming a gerontologist was coming true. I would be studying with some of the best minds in the world. I would go on to help improve the manner in which the elderly were being treated in the nursing home population. I would have a tremendous positive impact and, here's the important part, *everyone would think very highly of me*. Because of my "important work" with the elderly, I would be respected and admired. That's what I really wanted – to be respected and admired.

I came back to California to await my acceptance and make plans for moving to Chicago. Meanwhile, my job at the residential treatment home wasn't all it was cracked up to be. It was turning into a nightmare. Rather than counseling teenagers, the job was more about policing them. My primary responsibility, it turned out, was to physically restrain the boys, so they wouldn't hurt one another. They were constantly at each other's throats – literally. The leadership of the home told a great story to the outside world about the positive attention and counseling the boys were receiving. But as far as I could tell, the boys were every bit as out of control from one day to the next.

Working in an environment where everyone, residents and staff alike, disliked being there was something I hadn't encountered before. I found it was taking its toll on me. I soon began to hate my job. I didn't want to wake up in the morning because I knew the nightmare of going to work was going to start all over again. I grew to despise the leadership and management of the residential treatment home. I felt that they had lied to me about the job in the same manner that they were lying to the public about the "good works" they were doing for the kids. My only saving grace was I knew that I would soon be leaving for a much greater world.

Every night I went to bed with the feeling that the next day I would hear about my acceptance to Northwestern. I was told I would hear something in a matter of weeks, but two weeks went by and I still hadn't heard anything. Then another week passed. As my job was progressively getting worse, I began to get anxious about not hearing form the school. Finally, after another week I decided to call the school. The woman on the other end of the phone sounded confused as to why I hadn't heard from them. She asked me for my name and put me on hold. I remember she had a very pleasant manner and seemed to recognize my name which, of course, I took as a very good sign. *Boy, won't they be embarrassed when they find out that they forgot to tell me that I got in*, I remember thinking.

"I'm very sorry, Brian, but…"

My whole mind and body went numb. Anyone who has had to endure a major rejection (if you hadn't, you probably wouldn't be reading this book) knows exactly how it feels. First you go through denial: "They made a mistake and got my name confused with someone else…." Then negotiation: "I'll bet one of the students who got accepted will back out and they will be coming back to me…." Then anger: "Those jerks! How could they do this to me! They didn't even have the decency to call me. After all I've been through…." Then finally acceptance: "Okay, I'm a loser." Ironically, I knew about each of these stages because they were the same stages that a person goes through before death. An interesting fact I had picked up in my – now former – career as a gerontologist.

"Would you like my thoughts? You lie about everything."
June Gregory

Chris

Chris entered our offices and quickly sized things up. I could tell that he was not impressed. He was a sharp-looking guy, dressed in a very nice suit. He looked to be in his late thirties or early forties. I also observed his expression as he came into June's private office. Like many people, he was thrown off by her weight. But unlike most candidates, who quickly responded to her overwhelming warmth, the look on Chris's face told me that he strongly disapproved of June. This was not a happy guy.

"I was impressed with your résumé," June began cheerfully.

"Thank you. I'm not sure if you can really help me. I'm looking for a senior position as a vice president. Do you handle that type of search?" he said condescendingly.

"Yes, that's the position we talked about on the phone. Did you have any trouble finding our offices? I know the directions can be a little tricky."

"No problem. I found it just fine. I'm sorry, would you mind if I slipped out for just a moment? I just realized that I need to make a quick call. I'll be right back."

Before June could respond, Chris was out of her office.

"What an idiot! I can't believe that he's treating you this way, June. I'll go tell him you got a call and won't be able to finish the interview," I said. After everything June had done for me, it felt good to be able to stand up for her for a change.

"No, I don't want you to do that."

"But, June, this guy is awful."

"You know, Brian, when I met you for the first time, you weren't exactly a prize yourself. But I didn't ask you to leave. He's used to fancy offices and people who are in good physical shape. I don't blame him for being put off by our offices or by my appearance."

I was dumbfounded. The one time I get to stick up for June and she ends up criticizing me! I hadn't seen her put up with this kind of attitude from anyone. For some reason, she wasn't upset with this guy. As we waited for Chris to return, I realized that I was completely unable to predict how June was going to react to a situation. For the life of me, I couldn't figure this woman out.

Finally, Chris made his way back into June's office. He appeared to be very distracted. I got the distinct impression that he didn't want to be there.

"Tell me about your ideal position?" June asked.

"Ideal, are you serious?"

"Yes," June said enthusiastically.

"Ideally, I want to be retired in three or four years."

"And then what?"

"I'd play golf and do all the things I don't have time for now."

"Like what?"

"Oh, I don't know. Why are you asking?"

"It's my job to understand what you want most in your career and why you want it. I want to know what motivates you. How else can I place you in a position that will meet your needs?"

"Oh, I see. Well, I'm not sure. Maybe I would do some traveling."

"If you had enough money to retire, how much golf would you like to play?"

"I don't know. Maybe three or four times a week."

"Are you a good golfer?"

"I'm okay."

"Your ideal job would be to be independently wealthy so that you could play golf three or four times a week and maybe do some traveling? Did I get that right?"

"Yes, I guess so," he said, looking a bit flustered.

June sat quietly and very calmly read his résumé.

After what seemed like several minutes of silence, Chris asked "Did you want to ask me anything else?"

June looked up. "Yes, if you're just 'okay' at golfing, why would you want to spend so much of your life devoted to it?"

"Oh, for goodness sake, what kind of interview is this?" Chris was clearly frustrated. "If you must know, I enjoy golf. I want to be free to do whatever I want to do. I'm tired of working for the same stupid idiots I've spent most of my life working for! Is that the answer you're looking for?"

June was completely unflustered by his anger. "When you achieve your goal, where would you like to travel?"

"I don't know and I don't care! I just want to travel. I really don't see how that is any of your business."

"There is no need to get upset with me. Most of the people I meet enjoy talking about their dreams and aspirations."

There was another long pause.

Chris collected himself. "I'm sorry. I don't mean to get upset. It's just that I don't really know what I want to do once I'm retired. I just really want to be free from the grind of working. I'm tired of it. I keep seeing these guys who are a lot less intelligent and who don't work nearly as hard as I do making a lot more money. They are able to retire. I feel that I should be able to do the same."

"They retire so that they can play golf and travel?"

"Yeah, I guess so."

"Chris, I have to tell you that I'm disappointed. You seemed like such a sharp guy on the phone the other day."

"What do mean you're 'disappointed'?"

"I certainly understand your desire to be free. We all want to be free. It's just that your idea of what it means to be free is, to be honest with you, *pitiful*. I had the impression that you were a bigger man than that. But I was wrong."

"What does that mean?" Chris asked, his voice growing louder.

"I determine the measure of a person by how big his or her dreams are. If devoting all your energies and talents to playing a game that you're just 'okay' at and traveling to places you don't have any real desire to see doesn't qualify as pitiful, then I don't know what does."

Chris sat in his chair just staring at June. It looked like he was at a crossroads between getting up and leaving or breaking down and crying.

"I just don't want to work for such a jerk." His demeanor was beginning to soften.

"Now, there's an aspiration with some substance."

"I'm not sure I understand?"

"How would your career change if you suddenly found yourself working for someone who inspired you and whom you respected?"

Chris sat quietly again – like a defeated prize boxer. His shoulders were down and his spirit was clearly deflated. "That would be nice, June, but I can tell you, it's not realistic. I've been working for a lot of years and I don't see that kind of person out there."

"Have you been looking for them?"

"Well, no, not exactly."

"If you haven't been looking, then how do you know they don't exist?"

"I meet a lot of people and I don't know anyone like the person you are describing."

"I'll bet that if you stop and think a moment, at least one person who has those qualities will come to mind. I've built a business around placing exceptional candidates with those types of individuals."

"I think that's great, June. But I don't have the luxury to look for that type of position. I have a mortgage and a family to take care of."

"So do most of the candidates I've placed. Listen, Chris, your problem is not that you have financial responsibilities. Your problem is you don't believe you will ever have what you truly desire."

"Maybe you can tell me what I truly want. I can honestly say that I'm not sure I know."

"Your desire is to become a person you admire. You want to live the life you are capable of living: to be truthfully pursuing your dreams, have passion in your work life, to be proud of the man you are, to have your integrity intact, fight for what you believe in, experience the joy of a great accomplishment. You want to live to your fullest. Give it everything you've got. Then, and only then, will you have the freedom you spoke of."

Chris sat quietly. I could see he was taking in June's comments. "I didn't know I was coming in to see a philosopher, but you're right. That's a very different picture from golfing and traveling, isn't it?" he chuckled.

"Yes, it is."

"I'm not sure what to say, June. I mean, sure, it would be great to live like that. I just don't think I'm that guy."

"Why is that?"

"I don't know. I feel like I'm stuck. I work with some good people. They're not all jerks. The other vice-president I work with is a decent enough guy. It's not all bad."

"Have you ever heard the saying 'The problem with arguing for your limitations is that you might win'?"

"I'm just saying that my job is not all that bad. I made it sound worse than it really is."

"Chris, nothing 'bad' is all bad. Even in the very worst career stories I have heard over the years, there are some good things about the situation. Don't talk yourself into believing the pluses compensate for the negatives. They don't. You know it and I know it. I have to believe you are too smart a guy to fall for that line of reasoning."

Chris sat quietly then, "Yeah, June, you're probably right. Maybe I've just become so used to the situation that I'm not seeing it clearly. It could be that I am justifying the negatives."

"The anger and intensity you have toward your boss reveals the truth of how badly your career is going. You know the example of the frog in a pot of water?"

"No."

"It turns out that if you place a frog in a pot of boiling hot water the frog will jump out unharmed. But if you take the same frog and put it in a pot of cool water and slowly turn up the heat, the frog will not jump out. It will eventually die."

"I'm the frog?"

"Yes. Chris, your motivation and passions are dying. You've been aware of this for a long time. Your dreams are pitiful and your work life is in a constant state of hopelessness. I'm offering you a way out. It's up to you whether you want to take it or not."

Chris looked at me as if I could give him some kind of relief. "You're not going to get a better offer than that," I said.

"I just never had anyone tell me it was possible. I guess I've never really believed I could have the kind of career you described."

"What do you believe?"

"That's a good question. I think I've always believed I had to do what other people expected of me. That the only way anyone would respect me is if I did a good job doing what they wanted. That doesn't sound very good, does it?"

"It's honest."

"I'm not proud of living like this. I'm not sure I've really been aware of it until just now."

"Do you understand this one belief is controlling your career?"

"Oh, yeah, I see it. It's a little overwhelming," Chris said, while holding back tears.

"You want a sense of freedom in your career, is that right?"

"Yes, but that seems a long way off right now."

"It doesn't have to be. I can show you how to get it, but it won't be easy."

"I've never done anything the easy way, June."

"You're going to have to start giving yourself the very thing you've been working so hard to withhold."

"What do you mean?"

"Up until this point, you haven't received the praise and validation you need. You're going to have to learn how to give that validation to yourself. You're going to have to work hard to begin to make up for all the years you have been living under the false assumption you don't deserve or don't have the strength to go after what you really want."

"I'm just a little confused, what do I really want?"

"Why don't you take a moment and think about that question, then you can tell me the answer."

Chris sat for more than a minute thinking and then said, "I don't know if this is what you're asking, but it's what just came to my mind. There was this old movie called *Gentlemen's Agreement*. Gregory Peck plays this guy who won't compromise himself. I've always wanted to be a man like the character in that movie."

"Tell me more about the character."

"He's got a lot of inner strength. Yet he is kind and compassionate. He's not afraid to say or do what he believes in, even if it upsets everyone else.... That's it. He's the opposite of me. I do everything to please others. He does what he feels is right. He's true to himself."

"It sounds like he is honest with himself. He also has the courage to say or do the difficult thing other people are too afraid to do," June said.

"Yes, that's right."

"So let me ask you, if you could become the type of man Gregory Peck portrays in that movie, would you have the freedom you want?"

"That's a great point, June. Yes, I would. I guess that's really my dream: to be a man like him."

"Chris, you can choose to be that man any time you want. You can do it right now, this very moment, if you wish."

"How do I do that? I feel like I'm a long way off from being able to do that."

"You can start with this. Imagine for a second you are the Gregory Peck character. Now imagine you find yourself living in Chris's career. Do you have that image?"

"Yes, I think so."

"Now tell me what immediate changes would you make?"

"I wouldn't work for the same CEO I'm working for now."

"What kind of CEO would you work for?"

"I would work for someone I admired. Okay, June I see what you're getting at. Yeah, you're right. That is what I need to do. I need to stop making excuses for myself. Even coming here today, it wasn't to find a better CEO. I just wanted to see if I could make more money. I really do need to start being more honest with myself. I also need to have more guts. I know what I need to do. I think I've just lacked to courage to do it."

"It comes down to how you want to treat yourself. Because you have been treated as though you didn't deserve to have what you truly want, you never learned how to give those things to yourself. You see yourself as a weak, undeserving man. You make career choices which continue to reinforce that view. That is the story of your career so far."

"How do I change that?"

"So far you have been driven to choose leadership that will treat you in the exact manner you subconsciously believe you deserve to be treated. From one perspective, you could say you have done a very good job of finding leadership that will reinforce your poor self-image. To change that pattern, you will have to commit yourself to working hard at seeing yourself like the character in the movie. This is going to be difficult, but it can be done. The key is to know your dream well – know who you want to become. Then go out there and find leadership with those qualities. Find a work environment which will bring out the best in you. Commit yourself to finding leadership that will challenge you to become the man you ultimately want to become."

"I guess if I was so good at finding the wrong people to work for, I could become just as proficient at finding the right ones."

"That's true. However, the right leadership is much more difficult to find. So you're going to have to become very good at this in order to be successful."

Chris thought about that for a moment. "Yeah, I can see that I really have my work cut out for me here."

"If you set your mind to it, I have absolutely no doubt that you will be successful."

For some reason I didn't yet understand, when June gave encouragement there was an overwhelming sense of truth about it. You knew what she said was much more than just encouragement. It was reality just waiting to happen.

"June, I want to thank you. I really needed someone to call me out on my negatives. No one has ever done that for me. You're right, I did feel hopeless. I don't feel that way right now. I can't tell you how much I appreciate it."

"You're welcome."

"I want to become more honest and uncompromised. Someday I really hope to get there."

"You missed the point. This is not a 'someday' goal. This is your goal right now, this very moment. Don't get stuck in the idea that 'someday' you will be happy when you achieve this thing or that. Be that man right now. It's not about becoming that person. It's about choosing to act like that person in each and every moment, whether you feel like it or not. So many people lose their way by believing they will be fulfilled 'someday' when they are richer, more educated, have their own company, or go on vacation. For you it was early retirement. The list goes on and on. The truth is you will be happier when you choose to act like the man you want to be. You can choose to do that any moment of any day. Everything we desire in our work lives is available to us right now. The future has nothing for you. It's now or never."

"I have to say that I don't believe that I've met anyone who seems to have as much passion for her work as you do, June."

"I love what I do. I usually find a way to enjoy myself no matter what mischief I'm up to."

"Even if you were playing golf?" he asked.

"Even if I were playing golf," June answered.

They both had a good laugh. For that brief moment, Chris looked like a free man. He was smiling from ear to ear and June was, well, June.

"Now let me ask you a tough question, June. I know you said I keep seeking the quality of leadership that will treat me in the manner I feel I deserve to be treated. But since it doesn't make me happy, why do I keep doing it? Why does everyone I know keep doing it? How come no one seems to be learning from the same huge mistake?"

"Chris, in our own way, everyone is going after the same big prize in their career. The big prize is validation and fulfillment. We long to accomplish something that we are deeply proud of. We all long to hear the words 'you have done a great job' by someone we respect in authority. The problems in our career can all be traced back to those we choose to be that authority. Many of us have grown up with parents who were less than perfect. I know mine certainly had their limitations. Our parents are our first and most important authority figures. They are the first ones we look to for validation: to hear them tell us how proud of us they are. Even if our parents are not very good at validating us, we continue to look to them for that validation. We continue to bring our deepest needs and desires to them, even if they are not able to meet them – even if we are being completely ignored."

"Yes, that's exactly what happened to me. My dad was a strict disciplinarian. No matter what I accomplished, it was never good enough. He always wanted more from me."

"That's why you sought out and then chose to work for authority figures just like your dad. More than anything else in your career, you longed to hear the words, 'Great job, I'm so proud of you' from someone just like your dad. The problem is *because they are just like your dad;* you are no more likely to hear those words from your CEO than you were from your dad."

"That makes a lot of sense, June."

"The most important single lesson from our past is to not recreate the situations that brought us unhappiness in the first place. We get ourselves into these fruitless searches: If I can get my deepest needs and desires met from someone just like the person(s) I couldn't get them met by in my childhood, then and only then will I truly have what I want."

"So I have to find leadership who has the exact opposite qualities of my dad, right?"

"Just his negative qualities, I'm sure he also had some good qualities. The most important lesson anyone can take away from dealing with an authority figure who cannot meet their needs and desires is to stop looking to them as an authority figure. Find a new one who can give you what you want and need most. There is absolutely no success in going back to the same dry well over and over again. That will only guarantee failure."

"That's interesting, June. You're saying that I have been going to the same dry well because somewhere in my mind I have the idea that if I can get water from that well, it will taste better than a well that has an abundance of water."

"You got it."

"You realize that this changes everything?"

"I hope so."

"I've wasted so many years going to the same old dry well. This time I can't even blame my dad. He didn't make me repeat the same mistake."

"That's true, but just keep in mind there isn't something fundamentally wrong with you. You were chasing the same validation and desires we are all chasing. You were just off the mark. Like an archer with bent arrows – no matter how hard you work at hitting the target you are destined to miss. Not because you didn't try hard enough or care enough. You just weren't aware that your arrows were bent."

"Well now that you have straightened them out for me, I have no excuses. I'm going to hit the mark."

"And I will assist you."

"I know that I couldn't be in better hands."

The two of them chatted further about the position June had recruited Chris for. No longer focused on the salary, Chris wanted to hear June's impressions of the leadership. He was a completely different man than the person who had walked into our office 45 minutes earlier. As I watched him talking to June now, he was taking on the characteristics of his hero in the movie. He looked self-assured and, strangely enough, there was a real sense of kindness about the guy. This was the same guy who had been such a jerk. Did June somehow know this is who he really was? Is that why she didn't react negatively to him?

I was sitting in on these interviews because I was supposed to be learning how to interview. In truth, the only thing I was learning was I had no idea what June was going to say or do next. But the dream for my career was becoming clear: *I wanted to be just like her.*

On my long drive home I began to sort out all the thoughts and questions I had swimming around my head. It had been almost a month since I started working for June. It had taken me the entire month to figure out what Chris was able to realize in one interview with June. Up until this moment, I hadn't known what my dream had been. Here she was right under my nose every day and I hadn't known it.

How had I missed it? I started thinking back on the circumstances leading up to my first interview with June. That had been such an overwhelmingly difficult time for me. As I slowed down for the normal commute traffic, my thoughts drifted back to my life before I had met June. *What dreams did I have? What unresolved issues from my past had I been struggling with in my work life? And the biggest question of all, given all my fears, lack of confidence and anger at the time, how did I end up working for the boss of my dreams?*

Brian

After discovering I had been rejected from graduate school at Northwestern, I began to slip into a depression. I hated my job at the residential treatment center. I was married to a woman with whom I wasn't the least bit compatible – or in love with. I had a newborn daughter I cherished, but I felt utterly incapable of being a good father. I was full of fear. Fear of failing. Fear of abandonment. Fear of betrayal. Fear of life. Fear of myself.

Each day was worse than the last. With a degree in psychology and philosophy and a special emphasis in gerontology, it seemed to me, my degree was more confusing than it was marketable. I felt trapped in a job I despised and in a life that was overwhelming. My ultimate fear that I would end up a loser (the fear that had motivated me to do well in school) was beginning to become more than just an emotion. It was becoming a very real possibility.

It was during this period of depression that I arrived at two important realizations. The first one occurred on my drive into work one day. It came to me I had to take my rejection from graduate school and use it to motivate me toward a better life. I wanted to somehow get even with Northwestern for rejecting me. I knew the only way for me to do that would be to succeed in a big way. It didn't take a lot of brain power to realize my goal was way out of reach based on where I was at that moment. I knew it was going to take me a long time, perhaps even a lifetime, but I was determined to do it. Sitting in my car, I said to myself that someday I would be able to honestly say that I was grateful to Northwestern for rejecting me.

This new motivation lifted me out of my depression but, unfortunately, not for very long. The constant negativity I was experiencing in my work and personal life soon overshadowed any glimmer of motivation I was able to muster. Still, I was determined to fight back.

A second epiphany came days later while taking a walk. I was feeling particularly desperate that day and had left my house in hope of getting some perspective. In addition to my other problems, my daughter had become very ill and was in the Intensive Care Unit at Stanford University Hospital. None of the experts could figure out why she was so sick. Robin and I took turns staying at the hospital with our daughter. Neither one of us got much sleep. The stress on our relationship was tremendous. As new parents, we both felt responsible for our daughter's illness and the severe pain she was experiencing. After a month in the hospital she was finally declared healthy again and released. Then I received the bills from the hospital. They may as well have asked for a million dollars. I was flat broke. Everything felt like it was piling up on me. I kept wishing I would wake up and discover that my life was just a terrible nightmare. I wanted so desperately to escape from it all.

Then it hit me. I really needed help. I couldn't make it alone. I thought about everyone I knew and, sadly, I came to the realization not one of them could help me.

So I began to pray: "*God, please help me. Please bring me a person who will bring out the very best in me. I want to become my very best. I know it's in there.*"

I was not a religious person. In fact, I had never really prayed before. I wasn't brought up going to church, nor did I spend much time thinking about God. My prayer just popped out of me. I imagine it came out of nothing nobler than mere desperation. With that said, somehow I had a sense that it was right – and that it was heard.

My financial pressure was becoming increasingly unbearable. So when a friend suggested I come with her to apply for a higher paying sales position I agreed. I reasoned I was no longer really helping the emotionally disturbed boys. The truth, I realized, was I had become one. I went to the interview, except it really wasn't an interview. The man explained the job consisted of going door to door selling insulation. The local power company had started a program to reimburse customers who added insulation to their attics, and this company was selling and installing the insulation. The man explained while the company had nothing to do with the actual power company, most people would jump at the product. He also explained the job was a 100 % commission and that we would be employed as independent contractors, meaning we were not actually employed by the company itself. In other words, if you wanted the job you got it, good luck. End of interview.

My friend explained to me how much money a friend of hers had made selling the insulation. All I could think about was how much I needed the money and how much I hated my job. I decided to go for it. Giving notice to my manager at the treatment center was the greatest thrill I had experienced in a long time.

If you haven't done it, I can tell you that it isn't easy getting up the courage to knock on some stranger's door. The first one is always the hardest. I won't tell you selling insulation door to door was more difficult than restraining overly-medicated, emotionally disturbed teenage boys. But it wasn't easy. I hated the idea of bothering people in the middle of their dinner or waking them up from their weekend nap. Knocking on that first door of the day always created an awful feeling in my stomach. But there was an upside to this job. People were remarkably nice. I was constantly amazed at how many people treated me kindly. Sure, there was the occasional "get off my property or my dog will eat you" experience. But for the most part, people were respectful. And more than just respectful, a surprising number of them bought the insulation.

After making the sale I would take measurements to determine how much insulation the customer needed. Then the company would set up an appointment to install the product. I would get my commission after the job was completed. I was doing really well. I made enough sales that once I was paid, I would be in a good position financially for the first time since graduating college. Unfortunately, almost all of the installations I had sold were being delayed, and my bills were continuing to pile up. I wasn't too worried about this delay because my sales continued to increase. I was amazed and comforted by how much money I would be receiving.

Then I started getting calls from customers complaining the company had canceled the scheduled installation for the second or third time. When I would follow up on a customer's behalf, I kept getting the run-around from the company. One day I called and no one answered. The next day the phone was disconnected. The company was gone. My friend who had told me about the job explained to me the company was being run by a group of con men who, after collecting the money from the customers, closed shop and left town. She also explained to me we would not be receiving any of the commissions owed us. "Not a dime," were her exact words.

You might think I would have been really upset. But for some strange reason, I wasn't. Maybe since I had never made anything over minimum wage, the idea of making more money hadn't really sunk in. Or perhaps, I had just grown accustomed to failure. Or maybe I was just so happy to have left my previous job at the treatment center I really didn't care as much about my money problems as I had thought. Whatever the reason, I calmly came home. For the first time, I decided to pick up a newspaper and look at the want ads. I had no idea what kind of job I was looking for. I looked through the job categories and remember thinking how different they were from majors in college. There weren't any categories in psychology, philosophy, gerontology. Heck, there wasn't even anything in English, history or anthropology. It looked to me like the job world and the college world had absolutely nothing to do with one another. *I wish someone would have mentioned this to me while I was in college*, I remember thinking.

Secretly, I suppose I was looking for something that read: "Great high-paying job, doing meaningful work helping others. Candidates must have a degree in psychology and philosophy with an emphasis in gerontology. No experience, maturity or real talent required."

Instead, I saw only one ad that caught my attention. It read: "Personnel – call June 415-493-XXXX." That was it: three words and a phone number.

After my experience doing door-to-door sales, I found it rather easy to call the number and start talking. I don't remember what she asked me or how I answered, but I do remember we arranged for me to come in the next day for an interview.

I soon discovered that June's office was over an hour away from my house. Not a good start. Nevertheless, I wanted to follow up on the interview. After all, I reasoned, I had never had a real interview. And, to be honest, after all I had already been through in my short career, I really wasn't thinking much at all. I was just going through the motions. When I thought about my future, part of me was expecting to find a great job and the other part was expecting to be broke and homeless.

June's office was on the second story of a long and narrow office building. The hallway leading to her office seemed to go on forever. The corridor leading to her office was filled with State Farm agents, private detectives, bail bondsmen and the like. I walked into the office and was met by a receptionist. The office was no more than twenty feet wide and fifty feet deep. It was sectioned off by cubicles so I could not see anyone other than the receptionist. There were, it seemed to me, way too many plants. The walls were covered with all kinds of pictures of lions. The overall effect was that of some kind of small, odd 1970s-style urban jungle.

I sat down and started filling out an application. I was about halfway through when the receptionist asked if I was there to meet with June. When I replied that I was, she leaned over her desk and whispered to me, "She's nice, but I don't think she is very well – I don't think she has much longer to live."

Thanks again to my "I'm not really thinking about anything" state of mind, I didn't give the receptionist's comments or the unusual office décor much, if any, thought. I finished filling out the application and waited to meet with June. After a short wait, the receptionist indicated that June was free to see me. She then wished me good luck. But it was not the normal kind of "good luck." It felt more like the kind of good luck you would expect to be wished before jumping out of a plane for the first time or going in for major surgery.

An hour later, my first meeting with June was coming to an end. Despite the fact (or maybe because of it) she had called me "the most dishonest person" she had ever met; I knew that I wanted to work for her. I think I sensed June might very well be the answer to my prayer. This strange, powerful, joyful, scary, successful, full-of-life, honest, heavy woman might be the person who could fulfill my wish, my dream, to discover the best I had to offer.

I found myself practically begging for the job.

"I'm going to give you a chance, but for the life of me, I really don't know why," she said.

That's how I found my boss June.

Debra

While marketing to find clients, I hit upon a venture capital firm looking for a receptionist. They wanted someone who was very smart, who had a degree from a top school and yet would be happy working as a receptionist. The management, while being a little elitist about having an education from a top school – something they all possessed – seemed like very nice people. They were honest about the pluses and minuses of the position and were considered to be one of the top venture capital firms in Silicon Valley.

June and I talked about the position and decided I should recruit for it. As any headhunter would do, I began my job by calling the competitors of the venture capital firm. I then asked their receptionists if they could recommend anyone they knew for the position.

After about two hours of recruiting, I had two referrals. This turned out to be the easiest assignment I ever had. Because the receptionist was the person to answer the phone, I didn't have to work to get past the receptionist to the person I was trying to talk to. Also, I quickly discovered most receptionists enjoyed speaking to me, and many of them knew of friends who were looking for a good opportunity.

Both individuals who had been referred to me seemed to hit the mark. They had recently graduated from top schools. One was a UC Berkeley graduate and the other was from Stanford. Neither of them had any real work experience.

Debra, it turned out, had been looking for a job for the past two years. She had been working temporary positions while continuing to look for the "right" position. She came to the interview dressed casually. She didn't want to finish filling out the application until she heard more about the job. June picked up right away her attitude was less than positive. Nevertheless, she gave Debra the same joyful greeting she offered everyone who came to her office. After some brief small talk, June began the interview.

"So let me ask you, why didn't you want to complete the application?" June asked.

"I've been to a lot of agencies and, to be honest, I find that most of them are just a waste of time."

"Why's that?" June asked, staying remarkably calm.

"They don't listen to what I want and they just keep sending me out on positions I'm overqualified for."

"I see," June said looking at a section of her application that she had filled out. I see that you are looking for a position in graphic design. Did Brian explain to you that this position is a front office job?"

"Yes, but I thought they might have a need for a graphic designer as well."

"No, I'm sorry they don't. I certainly wouldn't want to treat you like the other agencies and send you out for a position that isn't what you are looking for."

"I don't understand. Don't you want to talk me into going out to the interview?"

"No, I wouldn't want to do that, but thank you for coming in."

"Well, I would be open to other types of jobs if you have them. Or do you just do receptionist positions? Of course, if you don't want to work with me, I can just go."

June sat up straight in her chair. "I can't help you because we are not working together. You're playing games with me in the same manner you claim other agencies have played games with you. I don't have time for games."

"What do you mean I'm playing games?" the candidate responded angrily.

"You come here for an interview, but you don't want to fill out the application. You have already determined we are a bad agency, yet you want us to help you. You haven't had a direct hire position in over two years, yet you resent the opportunities you have been given. I see here you are asking for a minimum salary that is ten thousand more than other recent college graduates, yet your unstable background and poor first impression are less marketable than candidates asking for far less money. You want a position for which you are not qualified, and you somehow believe that you are overqualified for the positions that you are qualified for."

"Is that all you have to say to me?" she asked incredulously.

"No, since you asked, it isn't. Your attitude is poor. You're rebellious and you are not dressed for an interview. You told me you didn't want to waste your time on positions that are beneath you. Yet when I tell you I can't help you, you act put off. You want me to tell you about the opportunities you just finished telling me you didn't want to hear about. So far you have lied, misrepresented yourself and been defensive. You have an attitude of entitlement, and you say one thing when you mean another. You are playing a game of 'I'm going to reject you before you can reject me.' That's what I mean by playing games. You are so afraid of being rejected you won't risk putting your best foot forward. That's how a coward acts."

"I didn't know that this was going to be a real interview, or I would have dressed more professionally," she said defensively.

"If you didn't think it was going to be a real interview, why did you bother to come?" June asked.

"Well, I have to eat, so I need a job."

I was amazed at how quickly she had transformed from a candidate who thought of herself as being "above" the job to a candidate who was absolutely desperate for any job. Because of her fear, poor attitude, and defensiveness she wasn't the least bit qualified for any good opportunity. I was beginning to grasp just how significant a person's attitude was in attracting the right job. I was also aware that I was much more like Debra than I cared to admit.

"You haven't answered my question," June said.

Debra thought about it a moment then replied, "I guess if I were you, I would have concerns about working with someone like me."

"Good, now we are getting somewhere. I'll make you this offer. You think about everything we talked about here today and when you are ready, give me a call. I'll set you up for another appointment and we can start over. We'll have a fresh start. How does that sound?"

I looked at Debra, expecting her to jump at the idea, but she didn't. She gathered her things and thanked June for the interview. To her credit, it seemed a very genuine "thank you." She told June that she would think about everything she had told her and get back to her. But something in me knew that she wouldn't. I wanted to take her by the shoulders and shake her. I wanted to tell her I was just like her and she could change her life in an instant if she really wanted to. I wanted to tell her she was sitting across from the one person in the world who could help her turn her life around if only she would let her help. There was so much I wanted to say. But instead I just watched her leave.

I sat befuddled in June's office. The whole thing with Debra felt like a waste. Not a waste of time but a waste of a life: a waste of potential. "I should have said something to her," I told June.

"Yes, you should have. You might have made the difference. Don't hold back if you have something to offer."

I thought about how different my life would be if June had decided to hold back on saying what was on her mind during my first interview.

"On the other hand, Brian, she wasn't open. Debra was so afraid of being hurt and rejected; she really wasn't looking for answers. That's the difference between you and her. You are open. You are looking for answers. You have a lot of negatives. Really, you have a lot more negatives than she does, but the fact you want to change is a plus. If you stick with it, it will bring you a lot of growth."

It was just like June to give me a compliment and then zap me by telling me that I was worse than the worst candidate I had ever met. However, I was so hungry for a compliment I chose to focus on the positive. I was in a good position because I was open to change. June said I was looking for answers. I liked thinking of myself that way.

"Your biggest plus is that you have nothing to lose. You didn't go to a good school like Debra. You didn't have people telling you that you could accomplish something worthwhile. You were at such a low point that you were hungry to learn," June said.

So much for compliments.

As I thought about Debra on the way home, I remembered an old joke a friend told me: "How many psychiatrists does it take to change a light bulb?" my friend asked.

"I don't know," I replied, waiting for the punch line.

"One, but the light bulb has to want to change."

Debra, at least for now, was not that kind of bulb.

"Do you realize that your arrogance is a cover-up for all your insecurities?"
June Gregory

Brian

Somehow I had gone from being called the most dishonest person she had ever met to being hired – all in one interview. The moment I acknowledged my dishonesty, I felt that she had completely forgiven it. She had wiped the slate clean. I was also aware that the instant I reverted back to my dishonest ways, she would pounce on me like a lion (maybe that explained all the pictures of lions in her office). She wanted honesty, and as long as I was not trying to hide *anything* from her, *anything* was possible – even the opportunity to work for her.

After leaving her office I got in my car for the long ride home. I was very happy with myself. The whole experience seemed surreal, but I felt I had come out victorious. I knew, deep within, that in meeting June something strange, yet very important had happened. I enjoyed the strange feeling for what seemed about a half hour. Then I had the vision of telling my family and friends about my new job and everything changed. I had just accepted another job as an independent contractor working without benefits for 100 % commission. *What was I thinking? Had June put me into some kind of trance?* The battle in my mind had begun.

June was right. I needed to learn how to be honest with myself or I would never be happy, no matter what I did with my career.

On the other hand, I needed and deserved to make money. It was unfair I had money problems. It was wrong that she was paying commission only. However, I wasn't exactly in a position to negotiate. Somehow I knew I had been extremely lucky to have a chance to work with June. No one had ever talked to me the way she did. If I wanted to learn how to be honest, if I wanted to stop constantly pretending to be somebody I wasn't in order to be accepted by others, this was my chance.

The mental battle continued all the way home, back and forth between my need for money and relief from my financial stress and this vague, but real sense that this was my chance to deal with my deeper problems. By the time I arrived home, I was exhausted from all the mental energy the interview and ensuing internal battle had taken out of me. I knew I was going to have to explain my new job to my wife, family, friends and the not-so-nice woman at the collection agency, but I didn't have it in me to get into an argument.

What was I going to tell everyone? I could just imagine the conversation: "Hi, guess what? Well you know how I just got ripped off from my last sales job working for 100 % commission as an independent contractor? And you know how I have this incredible financial burden right now as a result of that job? Well, you will be glad to know I've taken care of the problem. I just accepted a new job in a field I have no real interest in, working for 100 % commission as an independent contractor with no medical benefits. This job is different though. Rather than going door to door, I will be making cold calls all day for a woman who called me the biggest liar she ever met and whose own receptionist claims she doesn't have long to live. Oh, by the way, this job has a much longer commute."

Needless to say, I couldn't see the conversation about my new job going over very well with my justifiably frustrated wife, my degree-obsessed family, my save-the-world friends or my payment-hungry bill collectors. So I lied. I played dumb. I told them I was excited about the opportunity, which was true, and I hadn't ironed out all the details, which was not true. My strategy worked but not in the way I had imagined.

As I told them about my new job I could see on their faces they had an even lower opinion of me for taking a job without knowing the details than they would have for accepting another commission-only position. I was able to get away with a reaction that can best be summed up as: "He is just so stupid I can't get mad. I actually feel sorry for him." I was so thankful for not having to defend my choice I didn't even mind being written off as pitiful, stupid or insane. That's how I was able to avoid what would have been an intense and heated discussion with my family and friends.

Santa Cruz, California in the 1980s was – like Berkeley – one of the last strongholds of the hippie era. Almost everyone under the age of 60 preached love and peace but was very angry at the government, capitalism, and anything that had to do with the "establishment." This anti-establishment philosophy carried over to the dress code. Tie-dyed shirts, run-down jeans and sandals were standard wear. Even though I had become anti-anti-establishment while living in Santa Cruz, the politics and way of life had eventually made their way into my lifestyle. It was under these conditions I chose my clothes for my first day of work as a recruiter at Gregory and Leigh.

A wrinkled shirt, my best corduroy pants and (even now I find this difficult to admit to) sandals with socks. What a sight I must have been walking into June's office. When I arrived, June began my training by telling me more about the job. I would be on the phones, she explained, making cold calls to prospective clients who needed to hire a candidate. June ran a contingency placement firm which meant the employer paid a fee for hiring our candidate. There was no fee to employers for working with us unless they actually hired the candidates we sent them. After establishing a potential client, my next responsibility was to call possible candidates and recruit them for the job opening. I was responsible for interviewing the candidates I recruited and determining whether they were a good match for the client. We were matchmakers who did heavy telemarketing.

The key to the job, June explained, was the phones and my ability to stay on them. June explained to me when she was trained as a recruiter, the company she worked for gave her a copy of the yellow pages and a video about how to recruit. That was the extent of her training. She explained she was going to help me get started, and I could ask her questions if I needed more help. She made it clear, compared to her training experience, I was lucky to be able to ask questions.

The expectation was to make a minimum of 100 calls a day. She gave me a piece of paper marked with 100 numbered boxes. Each time I made a call I was to cross out a number. At the end of the day I was to turn in my paper and we would discuss my progress. That was the job.

"What Doesn't Kill You…"

If you have made cold calls (calling on someone you don't know), then I don't need to tell you how difficult a job it can be. If you haven't had the pleasure of cold calling, then allow me to explain the process.

The first call is always the most difficult. Your mind and body, at least in my case, relives the worst rejection you have ever experienced. For me that meant people laughing at me because of the severe speech impediment I had as a child. Before each first call every cell in my body felt the terrible ridicule I felt as a child. The second call was just a little easier than the first. By the tenth call my anxiety would decrease enough for me to realize I was sweating through my wrinkled shirt and my stomach ached. By the twentieth call, I might start feeling normal again. But then each day the process would start all over again. For me, the challenges of cold calling made going door to door look like child's play. In summation, I hated it.

June explained that for every nine "no" responses, I might get one "maybe." Starting out I might not get a "yes" for days, maybe weeks. My job was, in essence, to deal with rejection all day long.

If God could have personally designed a job that would best prey on my insecurities, he could not have surpassed what June had in store for me.

The one-and-a-half hour drive home each day was difficult. The mental battle raged incessantly. In those first days, I must have quit the job more than 100 times in my mind. All I could think about was I was driving three hours a day to a job in order to be rejected. No base salary so I could be rejected; no benefits so I could be rejected; ridiculed by my family and friends so I could be rejected. The torment would build on itself all the way home. But just before I would pull up at the house, something odd would happen. All the negatives about the job would subside and I would suddenly and strangely find myself beginning to feel good. Something deep within me was waking up, and it was an incredibly great feeling.

It was all about June. I felt great working for her. While I was sweating through my unimpressive, small wardrobe, I watched her do her thing. She was full of life. She was exactly as she appeared during our interview. She was strong, honest and, unlike me, she didn't seem to be afraid of anything or anyone. She spoke to her clients and candidates with a candor and strength I had never seen. I didn't like anything about my circumstances, yet I felt something I had never felt before: I was proud of myself for working for someone I genuinely admired. For the first time in my young work life, I was happy with myself.

Unfortunately no one else, especially June, was very happy with me. I was proving to be a lousy recruiter. My constant fear of rejection made me uncomfortable on the phones. In addition, I didn't have much fortitude. I would search for opportunities not to make the next cold call. I went to the bathroom at least ten times a day. I cleaned my desk five or six times (I only had four or five items on the desk). I continually asked June stupid questions to avoid making another call. I would take a break after each tough call. Who was I kidding? They were all tough! I would do anything and everything to avoid making my required 100 calls a day.

Once I actually gathered the courage to make a call, I wasn't very good. The potential clients and candidates I called could hear the fear and hesitation in my voice. I was anything but convincing.

June, on the other hand, was very convincing. She would spend time at the end of each day telling me exactly what I had done well (that part of the conversation went very quickly) and what I needed to improve on (that comprised the majority of our talks). As was her style, she didn't pull punches. She told me I had to learn to follow through my objectives each day and to stop living in fear of making the calls. On the other hand, she reassured me I could do it. Whatever she told me went right to my core. When she was giving me constructive criticism about my insecurities and fears I would think: *She's right. I'm so full of fear, I'll never succeed.* Then when she told me if I set my mind to it, I could succeed, I believed her. It wasn't that I just believed her intellectually. When June told me that she believed in me, for that brief moment, I actually felt successful – a feeling I had never experienced in my life.

Each day I received a psychological cocktail of June's cuttingly truthful observations of my weaknesses mixed with her remarkable ability to encourage me and genuinely believe in me. Incredibly, the cold calling began to get a little easier. As the calls got easier, I began to relax a little more with each passing day. Then one day about two weeks into my employment, another strange thing happened. The people on the other end of the phone began to sound friendly. The more calls I made, the friendlier they seemed to become. These were not the mean grownups who had laughed at me as a child. The companies and candidates I was calling were, for the most part, transformed into nice people who actually wanted to help me. People, it turned out, were nice. This was a revelation to me.

It remained difficult to make those first couple of calls each day, but I was getting over my fear of rejection and beginning to enjoy a new sensation I had not felt previously – or ever. I was beginning to have moments of confidence.

At the end of my second week, I sat down for our usual end-of-the-day meeting. June looked at my call sheet and saw that I was making more calls. "You are starting to make more calls. That's good. Every new recruiter needs to learn how to deal with rejection. It's difficult, but as you become more confident, you will find that it gets easier with time."

I sat and absorbed what she was saying. I was so proud of each and every call. I was pleased with my progress and the courage it had taken not to give up. I was basking in June's positive remarks.

Then June continued, "Your training is going to take a lot longer than I had imagined. I'm going to have you sit in on my interviews so you can learn this job. You are very insecure. You don't seem capable of being able to think straight for very long, and you are completely uneducated in anything to do with business. I can't figure out what, if anything, they taught you in college."

When I tried to argue and defend myself she would look me right in the eye and ask me with all sincerity, "Why do you continue to defend yourself? You lie. How are you going to grow if you are not going to be honest with yourself?"

Despite the overwhelming difficulty of hearing what she was telling me, something within me knew she was right and she wasn't trying to hurt me. Eventually, I would stop arguing with her. Rejection, it turned out, was not on the other end of the phone. It had relocated to June's office.

Get Over Yourself

Watching June interview candidates was fun and highly educational. The other benefit was that it took me away from the cold calling. We continued to have our end-of-the-day talks. She would offer her usual brand of praise and constructive criticism. I would go into each of these discussions with the commitment I was not going to argue or defend myself no matter what she said. Then she would come up with some new criticism I hadn't anticipated, and I would go off defending myself as vigorously as the time before.

"Brian, those clothes you wear show people how little you really think of yourself. If you went out and bought yourself a couple of nice outfits, you might start feeling better about yourself."

"Brian, why do you talk like you understand psychology when you don't even understand the first thing about yourself?"

I never knew what she was going to come up with next. She never criticized with malice, but she was always very clear and deliberate. After each comment I would think, *who is she to say that about me? After all I was successful in sports and school. I had friends who liked me. She, on the other hand, is overweight and over-critical. She may have been on target in our other talks, but she's wrong this time. Very wrong!*

Then, after a whole lot of explaining on June's part (she always explained her observations using metaphors and stories), I eventually would see her point of view. With some time, usually on my drive home, I would come to realize the deeper truth and meaning behind her comments. When these realizations hit me, I always felt stupid for giving her such a difficult time when all she was doing was trying hard to help me grow. Eventually, I would humbly thank her and renew my promise to myself not to resist her constructive criticism the next time she offered it. The cycle would, unfortunately, start all over again.

Listening to June interviewing, I began to appreciate her remarkable ability to see the truth about a person quickly and to communicate it effectively. It was a whole lot easier to appreciate her unusual talents when they were being applied to someone other than me. She had the uncanny ability to see the very best and very worst in a person. She also had the ability to use the exact right word to describe a candidate's qualities. Because of her incredibly benevolent nature and her ability to identify a candidate's best and worst attributes, most candidates actually listened to her without defending themselves.

I would sit there cringing as June would tell candidates they had a lot of unresolved anger and it was affecting their ability to choose a good work environment. I expected their response to be to jump across the desk and attack June with all the wrath of their "unresolved anger." But it never happened. They actually listened. And liked it!

I sat in on her interviews like a new painter observing the master at work. Candidates would sit quietly while she looked over their job histories. Then she would start her probing questions. She was genuinely fascinated by each candidate's career. I could see how much she really cared about them. I started to realize that she cared about them with as much passion as she was capable of telling them what was wrong with them. She would listen to their stories, their dreams, their frustrations and regrets. She listened to each word as if it was the most important thing she had ever heard.

Candidates felt comfortable telling June what they really desired in their careers. They also felt comfortable revealing to her why they weren't happy or how they had been cheated or betrayed by a manager or supervisor. She listened and observed. Then she would ask them what would seem to be a very innocent question (the same question she had asked me in my interview): "Would you like to know what I think?"

Then POW right between the eyes! She would hold them accountable – give them the big ugly. She told them, using exactly the right word(s), what was standing between them and their ability to achieve what they wanted in their careers.

"You act STUPID. I have to ask you, do you know that you are acting STUPID?"

"You are talking like a TEN-YEAR-OLD."

"You don't take RESPONSIBILITY for anything!"

"Do you realize that your ARROGANCE is a cover-up for all your INSECURITIES?"

"Why do you think you WHINE so much about your problems?"

I watched in total discomfort as she looked directly at candidates and told them the very worst thing about themselves. She always expressed the negative attribute I had been thinking about the candidate but would never have had the gall to communicate to their faces. Then just when I thought they would get upset, candidates would begin to pour themselves out to her. I could see, like me, they were relieved that someone finally said the truth out loud. Even though – or maybe because – what June had just told them was the most difficult thing they could have heard, they were not upset with her. Each candidate seemed to be thinking, "If this complete stranger can see this about me, then I guess *IT MAY NOT BE WORTH HIDING THIS PART OF MYSELF.*"

Then June would carefully put candidates back together. She would tie in how dealing with their negatives was the key to their growth. She would explain if they would take responsibility for their negative qualities and learn to be honest with themselves about those qualities, they could eliminate the frustrations they were experiencing in their careers. She would connect the dots between their inner world and their work life and give them a sense of power to make better choices. In turn, this would give them the opportunity to achieve what they truly wanted.

"What's the fun of having the money if you are so filled with insecurity that you can't enjoy it?" June would ask. "Why would you want to work so hard to become VP if you haven't learned how to respect yourself?" "Why are you working to retire when you don't know how to treat yourself well in the first place?" "Why do you think so much about career growth when you don't have the courage to take a risk?"

June knew that the key to career growth began with a person's inner world and was measured not by money, position, title or perks but by confidence, courage, fulfillment and the joy of achievement. The financial and professional growth that resulted from personal growth was an achievement to be proud of. And, most of all, June loved seeing people succeed.

Jennifer

My second candidate, Jennifer, came into the interview for the same receptionist position at the venture capital firm that Debra applied for. Unlike Debra, she was dressed in a very nice suit. June had me bring her back to her office where the three of us sat down. June began by complimenting Jennifer on her choice in clothing. It turned out she had bought the suit on sale at Nordstrom. The two of them talked about Nordstrom for the next 10 minutes while I sat there impatiently hoping the interview would proceed. My hopes were quickly dashed. It turned out that Jennifer was originally from Boston, June's hometown. That conversation was good for another 15 minutes while they each threw out names of the streets where they had lived. These long personal conversations June had with each candidate were driving me nuts!

After nearly 30 minutes of small talk, June got down to the business of interviewing. Since Jennifer didn't have any work history to go over, June started by going over her academic background and then asked her about her future.

"Ideally, what are you looking for?" June asked.

"That's a good question. I majored in English because I love to read and write, but beyond that I guess you could say I'm one of those lost souls who doesn't really know what she wants to be when she grows up. I had thought of being a teacher, but I'm not sure if that's what I really want or not," she said.

"I can understand that," June said empathetically.

With that reply, I knew June liked her. By now I had learned to determine whether June liked a candidate by how hard she came down on them early in the interview.

"What advice would you give me?" Jennifer asked.

"For most people it takes a while to recover from their college years. Especially if, like you, they have attended a top school like Stanford," June said.

"I'm not sure I understand."

"When you get out of college your intellectual level is up here." As June said this, she held her left hand up about eye level. "Your work experience is at this level." She held her right hand down at the desk. "The jobs that appeal to most people out of college are intellectually up here." June waved her left hand which was still raised. "The problem is in most cases, companies that claim to have entry level positions that require a high degree of intellectual challenge tend to be led by management whose capabilities are way down here." Again June put her hand down at the bottom of the desk.

"Yes, I would love a job where I can use my mind. Are you telling me that is unrealistic?"

"Yes, that's what I'm saying. The exception would be if your degree was in an area that made you highly marketable, like certain areas of engineering, for example. But with a degree in English, there isn't a lot of demand."

"Well, I have to admit when I looked at jobs, nothing really appealed to me. There just isn't a job title that jumps out at me. I mentioned I had thought of becoming a teacher but, to be honest, I don't see myself doing well with kids."

"If you don't enjoy working with children, chances are that may not be the right career for you."

"So then what?" Jennifer asked.

"The solution to this gap between your intellectual capability and your lack of work experience (again, June held her hands out visually demonstrating the gap) is to focus on working for leadership whose capability is up here in a job whose responsibilities may be down here," she said this time reversing her hands.

"I don't know if I could do that," she said.

June sat up in her chair, putting her arms down on the desk. I knew she was getting ready to make a point.

"Listen, the goal is to get your career to a point where your responsibilities match your intellectual capabilities." June held up both her hands to her eye level.

"Yes, that's what I want."

"The question becomes what is the fastest, smartest way for you to get there. Wouldn't you agree?" June asked a little more sternly.

"Yes."

"Here's the key. I want you to pay close attention. The first and most important thing you need to learn about your career is the overwhelming importance of working for good leadership. To work for people you respect and admire is the most important lesson in your career. If you learn that lesson at the beginning of your career you will save yourself from the frustration, poor choices and disappointment most of the world experience in their work life."

"But I don't want to waste my education just doing some entry-level job," she protested.

"You are missing the point," June countered.

"I guess I am," she said humbly.

"Let me explain it to you this way. Did you ever take a class in school in a subject matter you were very excited about, only to discover the professor was a real dud?" June asked.

(Yes, this professor metaphor June is about to talk to Jennifer about is the same one I used with Mark in the first chapter. Where else would I have gotten it from?)

"Yes. It was a class in American literature," she answered.

"What happened? Did you enjoy the class? Did it increase or decrease your interest in the subject? Did it increase or decrease your motivation and desire to learn? Did the class seem to go fast or drag out?"

"It was awful! By the end of the class I didn't want anything to do with American literature. I lost all interest in the subject. It seemed like class took forever to end."

"Now, conversely, did you ever take a class you really didn't want to take, but the professor turned out to be fantastic?"

"Yes, it was a class in statistics. I hated math."

"What happened there? Did it increase or decrease your desire to learn? Did the class go fast or slow? Did you enjoy going to class or begin to resent it?"

"No, I ended up loving that class. The professor was very funny. He was an amazing teacher. He made the whole experience a very positive one. By the end of the semester, I actually found myself enjoying statistics. If you would have told me I would like a math class, I would have told you that you were crazy. But he somehow made the whole thing interesting and fun. I was very proud of myself for finishing the class with an A. I really didn't think that was possible," Jennifer said.

"That's the secret of career growth," June replied.

"I'm not sure what you mean."

"In school it's the quality of the professor, not the subject matter which most greatly determines our desire to learn and grow. It's also what most greatly contributes to our sense of overall fulfillment. In our work lives, it's the same thing. It's the leadership of a company that will have the greatest impact on our motivation, growth and fulfillment. Not the level of responsibility. Not the pay. Not the promise of growth," June explained.

"I guess that makes sense," Jennifer said. But I could see she wasn't quite convinced.

"The great news about your work life is you get to pick the professors! You choose your teacher. Imagine being able to go through college with the freedom to choose classes solely on the basis of the quality of the professor. Wouldn't that be fun? Can you image how much more you would have learned? Can you imagine just how much more interesting school would have been?"

"That would have been amazing. I would have loved that! The funny thing is, given how much I liked my statistics professor and how much I learned from him, I probably would have ended up a math major. I would have taken every one of his classes."

"Are you seeing my point, now?"

"You're saying it doesn't matter what industry I work in or what job I do so long as I like the person running the company," she answered.

"Not just 'like' but, ideally, feel really inspired by. You didn't just 'like' your statistics professor, you were inspired by him. How else can you explain wanting to take more math classes when you hated math?" June asked.

"You're right, that's the word. I was inspired by him. It never would have occurred to me I could look for that kind of experience in my job search. Does that really exist out there?" she asked.

"Imagine that a person who was just entering the university asked you the same question. What if a freshman came to you and asked: 'Are there any really great, inspiring professors at this school?' How would you answer that?"

"I would tell the student, 'yes there are, but they are very rare.'"

"That's the answer to your question. Yes, inspiring leaders are out there but, just like in school, they are very rare."

"So how do I go about finding them? Can you tell me what companies have that kind of leadership?"

"Better than that, I can show you how you can find them," June said.

"I'd love to learn that!"

"Let's go back to that imaginary conversation between you and the freshman. How would you answer the same question in that case?"

"That's difficult. I guess I would tell them that when they first met their professor to trust their instincts."

"How can you trust your instincts, if you're not sure what you're really looking for in a teacher?" June asked.

"That's a good point. I guess I would first need to tell them what to look for in a great teacher."

"What would you tell them?"

"I would tell them to look for a teacher who enjoyed teaching. I would look for a good sense of humor, but I suppose that's not the most important thing. I think it just comes down to some teachers seem like they don't really want to be there – they are the worst! I would tell them to avoid a teacher like that at all costs," Jennifer offered.

"You're describing what they should avoid. Remember, you were telling them what they should look for."

"Okay, right, let me think." Jennifer thought about it and then a light bulb seemed to go off in her head. "Great teachers have a passion for teaching and really know their subject matter. They are great communicators, they're fair and they take a real interest in the students. I think that about sums it up," she said proudly.

"I'd say you summed that up very nicely."

Jennifer sat quietly for a moment. She appeared to be deep in thought. "That's it! That's what I'm looking for in a job. I want to work for someone like that. All these years I've been asking myself: 'What do I want to be when I grow up?' I've never really known. I thought there was something wrong with me. I mean so many of my friends have always known exactly what they wanted to be. They're so clear about it. I haven't known until this very minute. It's simple really. I've always wanted to be a part of something I really believe in. To work for people I admire, respect and, as you say, am inspired by. Like my statistics professor. I would have done anything to take more of his classes. But I talked myself out of it because his classes were not in my major. How stupid! Who cares his classes weren't my major? I learned more from him than all my other professors combined. And not just about statistics. He taught me about life: how to enjoy what you're doing; how to be really involved and engaged with other people; how to combine your passions with your life and work. I can't believe it's taken me this long to see this. It was sitting there right before my eyes all this time!" she exclaimed.

Now it was my turn to be impressed and a bit embarrassed. I was tracking the conversation up until this point, but as Jennifer expressed herself I realized I still hadn't fully grasped what June was up to with the candidates. I felt embarrassed I was just now getting it, despite having sat in on so many interviews.

"Those friends of yours who have always known exactly what they have wanted in their careers have a very important and difficult lesson in front of them. Like you, someday they are going to come to the realization that what they do for a living will not bring them the fulfillment they truly desire. We all have a deep desire to become the very best we can be. That's what it means to live your life fully. That's what it means to be truly successful. Becoming the best person you were designed to become is never a matter of what you do for a living. Becoming your best, realizing your potential as a person is a question of WHO you become, not WHAT you become. That's why who you choose to work for, the leadership, is far more important than what you choose to do for a living," June concluded.

"Is that always true, June? I know some people who are doing exactly what they have always wanted to do and they seem very happy."

"Either they understand what we are talking about and have made smart choices or they simply got lucky. I'm guessing that they got lucky. As they go through their careers, they will continue to emphasize the wrong priority in their job searches. They will focus on the job duties, money, title, or promises of growth. As they continue to do that, they are going to pay less and less attention to the deeper issues of relationship and leadership."

"That's true. My father's a doctor and I've watched him become increasingly dissatisfied with his career as he has gotten older. He doesn't get along well with his partners. It seems like all he cares about these days is making more money so he can retire earlier. He used to love being a doctor," she said sadly.

"When you look at people's careers, you will find they are less fulfilled over time. That's unfortunate and unnecessary. Right out of school, we have fewer needs so we tend to pay more attention to our instincts about the quality of people and leadership. But as we grow older our needs around money, security, status, and what other people think of us increase, and we pay far less attention to our deeper desires and instincts. We compromise and get into situations we know are not right for us. It takes courage to stop compromising. The truth is most people give in to fear and then wonder why they are not happy."

"That's exactly what is happening to my dad. I think he thought that as long as he was working as a doctor, he would be happy. When things went sour, he didn't do anything about it."

"Show me any job where the person in it is afraid to do what he or she knows is right, and I'll show you an unfulfilled, unhappy person. It doesn't matter if you're an attorney, doctor, clerk or actor. They may be growing financially, but they are dying soulfully. In fact, the more money they are being paid, the faster they are dying. There isn't a human being alive who can grow toward true potential in a work environment where fear and compromise are the driving forces."

"What about people who take jobs for the sake of their kids or families?" Jennifer asked.

"That's a good question. I said an environment driven by fear and compromise. A person can be in a bad environment and not be driven by fear and compromise if they have chosen to be there for the sake of a greater cause. That's an environment they believe in because it provides for their deeper needs. They can work for poor leadership and still grow because they have made a choice to be in that environment for a reason that is more significant than the negative effect of the job."

"That's a little confusing. How do you know if the reasons for working there are more significant than the negatives of working for poor management?"

"The true test of those situations is the degree of inner fulfillment the sacrifice is bringing to the individual. There is a fine line between being a martyr and a hero. Your father is martyring himself; that's why he is so unhappy. From what you have told me, he doesn't have a good reason, yet alone a significant one, for being in a bad environment. On the other hand, the gentleman who removes my trash every week is one of the happiest individuals I know. He always has a big smile on his face. He doesn't work for great leadership, he is not inspired by his boss, but he is taking care of his family in a manner he is very proud of," June explained.

"It sounds like you've spent some time talking with him."

"Yes, we've talked and he is looking for a job where he can feel more respect for the people he works for. He has not just accepted the fact that he has to compromise. That's important. But until that new opportunity presents itself, he is grateful for what he has and proud of how he is providing for his family. He is a man of honor. I expect some day he will be working for better leadership. In fact, I'm going to make sure that he does!"

"I'd like to be like him. I want to feel like my reason for spending forty hours a week at a job has significance for the people around me and brings a smile to my face as well. I've really got a lot to learn. But I trust you, and I'd love to go on this interview if you think this position could be that kind of opportunity."

"That's the spirit. I can't assure you this position is the right one for you, but that's what we will find out as you go through the interview process."

"You know, June, I came in here today wondering what I wanted to be when I grow up. I think I found my answer."

"What's that?"

"I need to grow up. I mean, I need to take my career and my life more seriously. I've just been going through the motions of trying to find a job. I haven't given any thought to the kind of person I really want to become or the kind of people I want to work for."

Before Jennifer left, she and June resumed their conversation about Nordstrom. I wasn't paying attention, but it seemed Jennifer was going to check out some item June was interested in and get back to her with the information.

I found myself marveling at how masterfully June had guided Jennifer toward knowing what she wanted to do with her career. She had come into the office without any direction. Now she was focused on what she wanted. An hour ago she lacked confidence and appeared to be completely unsure of herself. More than that, she was tortured by the sense there was something deeply wrong with her because, unlike her friends, she didn't know what she wanted to do in her career. Now she was clearer, confident and for lack of a better word, happy.

I was excited because I now had a very motivated, place able candidate. And all I had done was sit there like a bump on a log, nodding my head every time June said something profound. The candidate must have thought I was simply agreeing with June when, in reality, I was the last one in the room to comprehend what was going on.

Brian

As my first weeks slowly turned into my first months, I continued to spend my days on the phones recruiting for June's clients. I sat in on most of her interviews which allowed me to watch as she masterfully encouraged and dissected the candidates. Occasionally she would interview individuals who resisted her attempts to get to the root of their problems. Then she would ask me to try to explain the point to the candidates. Strangely, I was beginning to do a pretty good job of "translating" June to candidates who couldn't appreciate what she was trying to tell them. I was uniquely qualified as a translator. I was an expert in the language of emotional resistance, and I was beginning to understand June's language of honesty and strength. I was sympathetic toward the candidates' defensiveness and was able to encourage them to be open to what June was trying to tell them. Thanks to June's wisdom and my in-depth experience with fear and thick-headedness, we were slowly and strangely becoming a good team.

After an especially long day of recruiting, June asked me into her office. "You've been doing a good job lately," she began. "I've been invited to join a friend of mine on her company's bus for a trip to Reno. I thought you could use the break, so I'm inviting you to go."

My mind went immediately to the cost of the trip. "June I'd love to go (I really was very flattered that she was asking me to go), but I have so many bills. There's no way I could afford it."

As I was telling her about my financial problems, I began feeling conflicting emotions. On the one hand, I felt like a hero for doing the right thing; on the other, I felt sorry for myself that I was so in debt.

Once again something told me that June could see exactly what I was feeling.

"You know, Brian," she began "you are never going to be successful if you don't learn how to start treating yourself better."

"But, June, you don't understand. I am treating myself better by paying my bills and trying to pay off some debt." Even as I responded with an argument that made perfect sense, I was still aware of feeling sorry for myself for being in the predicament in the first place. I wanted these feelings to go away. I was tired of feeling frustrated, like a victim of circumstances. I knew she could see it. I wondered how I could make so much sense and yet not feel good about it.

"Let me ask you a question. Do you have fun at anything? Do you do anything just for fun?" she asked.

Now I felt defensive. Thoughts began to race through my mind: I have fun at a lot of things. I'm a really fun person. In elementary school, I had great friends. We'd play army, football and baseball in the streets until late at night. We'd build go-karts and forts. In junior high school, I was the guy everyone wanted on their team. In high school, my friends and I had all kinds of fun. Even in college, my buddies and I had some good times together.

But the more I thought about June's question (or accusation), I began to realize that in the two years since having been married and then having a child, I hadn't had any kind of fun. I was 24 years old now, and I had not had fun in a long time.

"Well, I used to have fun in sports and I had fun as a kid," I told her.

"How long has that been?" she asked.

"It's been a while. A good while," I admitted. "But, June, you've got to understand. I really don't have the money. I just don't have it. My wife would kill me if I told her that I was going to spend money on a trip to Reno."

"Brian, until you start learning to take care of your own needs, you are not going to take care of hers. From what I can tell, you are not doing a good job of taking care of her needs at all. Listen, nobody likes a martyr. You want to grow? You want to learn how to make a better life for yourself and your family? You are going to have to learn what you need in order to feel good about yourself. For starters, you need to dress better and get a haircut. And you need some spontaneity! If you are not willing to invest in yourself, you are not going to grow," she concluded.

I really walked into that one, I thought. I had heard what June said, but I still felt like what she was explaining was for other people – people who had money to pay their bills. It was for normal, responsible-type people, not for losers like me. Nevertheless, in order to keep the peace, we finished the conversation with me agreeing to talk to my wife about the trip.

Predictably, the talk with my wife that evening did not start off well. It must have been obvious to her I was asking her for something I really didn't want to ask for or was afraid to ask for. I was asking her only to keep my promise to June. I was, in fact, counting on her to say "no." But after my poor start at the conversation, a strange thing happened. As she raised the exact same concerns I had raised with June about the costs, I found myself repeating almost word for word June's points about why it was important to go. At first, I was just saying the words. But the more I repeated June's point of view to my wife, the more I started to understand what June had been getting at. And the more I began to understand what June had been trying to tell me, the more committed I became about the trip. It was weird. I was playing June, and my wife was playing me. Only this time I could see clearly how rigid and negative my point of view was. I could see how I had been arguing for my own limitations. I could see how I had, as June said, become a martyr.

It hit me that the way I was living was like a car trying to get somewhere on an empty tank of gas. I was constantly trying to perform better at work and at home, but I wasn't filling the tank. I had been running on fumes for a long time. It was no wonder there wasn't any spontaneity in my life. No wonder everything felt like a chore.

Finally, I even found myself passionately trying to explain to my now dumbfounded wife it was absolutely necessary for me to spend money in order to go to Reno. "If I don't learn how to take care of myself, I'll never have the energy or motivation to grow," I told her. If I hadn't been working so hard at trying to convince her of my point of view, I would have felt sorry for her. She had seen my attitude go from "I don't even want to ask you this" to "I've got to have this" all in a matter of seconds. As I saw the look of total confusion on her face, I wanted to tell her I hadn't understood why it was important for me to go either. But it was too late for that; I was too busy making by point.

Eventually she acquiesced and agreed I should go. I don't think she actually believed or understood anything I was trying to explain. Instead, after the sudden unexplained intensity I brought to our conversation, I believe that she was sold on the idea of a weekend away from me. I couldn't say that I blamed her.

With a little over $20 in my pocket, I was headed to Reno. June had several friends who worked at a local medical device company. Each year the company put together a trip to Reno for their employees and their friends. As I boarded the bus for the five-hour trip, I was immediately struck by the care-free, party attitude of the other passengers. Everyone seemed to be laughing and having a good time and the bus hadn't even left the depot. June, her two friends and I found our seats and got comfortable. I felt like a fish out of water on several accounts. I was at least 10 years younger than any other passenger. Other than June, I didn't know anyone. They were all having a great time, and I had forgotten how to have one.

Several of the people seated near us tried to engage me in conversation, but I was still too uncomfortable to find anything to talk to them about. The laughter got louder as everyone started drinking and telling their favorite jokes. I looked over at June to see her reaction and was surprised to find her laughing as vigorously as anyone on the bus. I had the sneaking suspicion she didn't understand all the jokes but was finding the whole thing funny anyway.

Eventually I became frustrated at myself for feeling like such an outsider. I was just sitting there finding anything I could think of that was wrong with the situation: That joke was dumb. She looks weird.

He's drinking too much. And so on. Then the passenger sitting opposite me told me her favorite joke. I don't remember what it was, but I do recall thinking that it was ridiculously stupid. And for some reason I do not understand, I began to laugh. And I kept laughing. The stupid joke suddenly seemed like the funniest thing I had ever heard.

And as I laughed, other passengers started to laugh with me. Suddenly, my feelings of being an outsider began to disappear. After I finally composed myself, I found myself talking to the people around me. It turned out they were really interesting and incredibly friendly. I even told them a couple of my favorite jokes. They not only laughed, they howled. The more they laughed, the more jokes I told. We were all having a great time.

Eventually, we all ran out of jokes. The laughter and storytelling gave way to a peaceful silence as one by one the passengers began to fall asleep. Personally, I wanted to keep going. I wanted to hear more jokes and talk to more of my new friends. It occurred to me that I had wasted the first hour or so judging everyone. How could I have been so completely wrong? This was the friendliest group of people I had ever met. As I looked around the bus looking for someone to talk to, I realized that it was too late – they were all out cold. Soon after, I fell asleep, as well.

The next sound I heard was one of the passengers yelling, "Reno!" I woke up to the bright lights of "the biggest little city in the world." As we pulled up to the hotel everyone was wide awake and anxious to get off the bus. When the bus doors finally opened, my new friends were gone so fast I wasn't sure what had happened. June was gone too. I wandered into the casino and found June playing on the slot machine closest to the entry. She hadn't taken three steps into the casino before sitting down at the machine. June had mentioned to me she enjoyed playing the slots now and then. But by the manner she had attacked the first machine; I knew this was more than just a passing fancy.

I took a seat next to June and began to take in the scene. I looked around for any familiar faces from the bus, but they must have scattered to the winds. I asked June about checking into our rooms and getting the luggage. She told me it was a good idea to take care of those things and she would be through in just a few more minutes.

Three hours later I was still seated at June's side while she continued to play the slots. My job was to collect the coins when she won a jackpot and stack them onto the plastic money racks. I didn't mind helping her out. In fact, it was fun. Each time she pulled the handle I would root her on. June played the slots the way she worked and in the same the way she dealt with me – she gave it everything she had. For some reason, she absolutely loved playing the slots and, not surprisingly, she was winning. From what I could tell, she was winning quite a bit.

Another two hours went by and I had stacked up a number of plastic trays all full of money. It was now the wee hours of the next morning, and I was exhausted. June appeared to be fresh as a daisy. She seemed to have limitless energy. As I began to wonder if there was going to be an end, or even a break, June announced that the machine had "cooled off" and we should check into our rooms.

After getting our rooms, June told me that she wanted to treat me to dinner for being a good sport while she was gambling. Since it was now around four in the morning, I was exhausted and not at all hungry. Instead of telling her how tired I was, I told June I was sure the restaurant was closed and we could go later when they were open. "Nonsense, they will be open. Come on," she said and off to the restaurant we went.

I hadn't realized nothing ever closed in Reno. The hotel restaurant was full of other people enjoying their 4 a.m. dinner. June and I took our seats and looked at the menu. The second I began reading the items, I realized I was starving. I ordered a steak, fries and a big, chocolate milkshake.

While we waited for the food to arrive, June told me when she was a night club singer she and the band would typically go out for dinner together. Since they didn't finish until one or two in the morning, they would eat around this same time. "It was fun. We would work all night and sleep during the day. You get used to it."

"In those days," June added, "all the big clubs in New York and Chicago were owned by the Mafia. I didn't like those guys one bit. One time after a show, I was eating with some of the band members and a hot shot walked into the restaurant dressed to the hilt. He recognized me from the show and came over to our table and started talking to me. He told me he liked the show and then made a crude overture toward me. I stood up and told him no one talked to me that way, and he needed to learn some manners. Then I reached down to my plate, picked up my omelet and threw it at him! I was very naïve in those days. It turned out this man was Dutch Schultz, the head of the Chicago syndicate. This guy had people killed for just looking at him the wrong way. Here I was with my omelet all over his expensive suit."

"So what happened?" I asked.

"Well, I don't mind telling you I was afraid for my life. But, fortunately for me, word got out he not only didn't mind my throwing the omelet on him, but he was asking around about me, showing an interest. When I heard that, I avoided the guy like the plague. But I still say he shouldn't have talked to me that way. I don't care who he was."

"How did you get started singing?" I asked her.

"I was always singing as a kid. I would walk up to complete strangers and ask them if they wanted to hear me sing. Before they could answer, I would just start singing. Then I would ask them for a penny. I was absolutely fascinated with myself," she said laughing. "If no one was around to hear me sing, I would stand in front of the mirror and watch myself. I thought I was absolutely great.

"My father, however, didn't like it at all, so I had to sneak around. I was terrified of him. If he caught us doing something wrong, he would smack us. I grew up one of eight kids and we were all afraid of him. My mother was great. She was always trying to protect us from him. She was very loving. We were raised Pentecostal, which is a very strict denomination. I grew up believing that I was going to hell for anything I did wrong. For example, the church believed if a woman wore lipstick, she was going to go to hell. If you drank alcohol or kissed a man before marriage, you would go to hell. It was awful.

"As a young girl, I was always the one getting into mischief. I was living in fear that my father would catch me and beat me, but it never seemed to stop me. When I was about sixteen, I heard about a talent show in downtown Boston where I grew up. Of course, I had to go. It never even occurred to me I could lose. I talked my sister into helping me sneak out of the house while my father was away. I ended up winning the show.

"The next thing I know I'm sneaking out of the house to go sing in clubs. I lived in constant fear for my life. I was sure if my father ever found out what I was doing, he would kill me. I mean really kill me. I was dressing up and putting on make-up and singing in bars. All the things he despised."

"How did you learn to sing?" I asked.

"I never took lessons. I just had my own style. I wasn't the best singer, but they said I sang with a lot of feeling. Of course, I believed I was the best singer who ever lived. I was just brazen that way," she said laughing.

"After a while my father began to suspect something was going on, but my mother continued to protect me. Eventually, I moved away from home into an apartment with my sister. But I continued to live in fear. Besides being terrified of my father, I was scared that I was going to go to hell."

"How come you hardly ever mention your singing background, June?"

"It's my weight. In show business, you are always concerned with your appearance. I'm embarrassed that someone will find out that I am the same June Gregory who used to sing. I don't like to talk about it much anymore."

"I know in our first interview, you told me a little bit about it, but how did you end up putting on the weight?" I asked.

"I really believed that if I kissed a man, then I had to marry him. That's what I grew up with. As a singer, you have men pursuing you all the time. After going through three divorces, which I also thought I was going to hell for, I just decided the only way to keep men away was to put on weight and make myself unattractive. I'm paying a big price for it. But I enjoy the freedom it's given me. I picked men who were like my father. They were always trying to control me. I just never learned how to choose the right kind of man. That's why it's so important to understand yourself well enough not to repeat your past," she concluded.

As I sat there in the wee hours of the morning, eating great food and listening to June, I realized I was completely relaxed and enjoying myself. For the first time in as long as I could remember I wasn't worried about anything. Not anything at all. Then it hit me. Since my teenage years, I had not experienced any real joy in my life. All I had known was the pressure of finishing school, the constant fear of surviving and making money, and the unhappiness of an unfulfilling marriage. I realized that my whole life, my every waking moment, revolved around my fears. I went to school out of fear, got a job out of fear and had married out of fear. I was afraid of people and of money. I was afraid of being a father, a husband and a provider. In short, I realized that I was afraid of everything and everyone. At the core of it all, I felt completely unqualified.

It was no wonder that I hadn't experienced any real enjoyment in my early adult life. Between my fears and poor decisions, I had carved out an existence completely devoid of any real joy.

But that night in the restaurant listening to June, I was free. Something in me began to come back alive. I had been given a glimpse of what my life could look like without the constant pressure of feeling like a failure. I could have joy again like I did as a boy. Fun and adventure could be part of the landscape of my adult life. It was possible.

After dinner we went to our rooms and slept until the afternoon. Around 5 p.m., June was back on the slots with me at her side. This time the slots were not so generous, and she was losing quite a bit of money. The more she lost, the more she concentrated on the machine. She had a real game face on, but she never complained. She just kept putting money in the machine and pulling the handle. "It's bound to pay off," she told me.

As I sat there I started looking around at the other gamblers. I noticed that most of them had a look of desperation with an occasional shout of relief when they won. June, on the other hand, wasn't at all desperate. She was very determined, but in no way was she desperate. In addition to her fierce determination to win at the slots, there was a sense of decency about June. She was like a child working very hard at winning a game. She was giving it her best, not because she needed to win, but because she really wanted to. Somehow, this was really fun for her.

Then it started. Slowly at first, but then in bunches. The machine started to pay, and it wouldn't stop. June was hitting jackpot after jackpot. Soon she was playing two machines at a time. It seemed to me when one machine wasn't paying the other one would hit. I was busy collecting the coins and stacking them into the plastic trays. We were on a roll.

Soon I assumed a new responsibility. I was taking the trays of coins to the cashier and cashing them in. Each time I brought June back a stack of cash, she would point out we needed to win enough money to fill up the trays again. She was glowing. As she continued to win, she attracted a crowd of people around her. My job expanded again. I was now the protector of the winnings.

The machines eventually cooled off. I was exhausted from having stayed up all night the previous evening, but June was still going strong. After another hour or so, she was ready to call it a night. I don't know for certain how much she had won but, as close as I could figure, it was well over $10,000 in all.

I fell into a deep sleep that night. In the morning, we had breakfast and talked about the placements we were working on and what was going on with members of her family. Eventually, we started talking about me.

"Do you understand why I wanted you to go on this trip?" she asked.

"Yes, because I need to start learning how to treat myself better," I responded. I had been so relaxed from breakfast and from the trip in general that my mind really wasn't working. I had just told her what I thought she wanted to hear. The truth was I really didn't know how to put into words what I had experienced on the trip. I just felt happy and relaxed.

"It's more than that," she began. "Life can be a struggle. Look at how hard you have been working lately. If you are going to learn how to be successful, you will have to bring some balance to your life. If all you know is hard work and pressure you will eventually burn out. You must learn how to have fun. You must learn how to enjoy your life. Balance is the key."

"Listen" she continued. "I appreciate everything you did in helping me with the coins. You were a big help."

June then reached out her hand and handed me two $100 bills. Since the trip had only cost me $100. Her gift meant I would be returning home a winner too. Not only did I have a blast, but I had managed to make money at it!

I could not explain the incredibly good feeling that came over me that morning. As we were walking out of the casino to board the bus home, I stopped by a slot machine. It was a five dollar machine usually reserved for the high-stakes players. I decided to play one coin. I put in my $5 coin and pulled the handle. Two cherries came up. I had won $5.

At the exact moment my coins were hitting the tray, a man walked by and introduced himself to me. His name was Ali, and he was in charge of the casino. He handed me his card and told me that anytime I wanted to come back to give him a call and he would "take care of everything."

I took my two coins and found June to tell her the story. "He must have thought you were a high-stakes player," she said laughing.

"You can never be yourself when you are feeling intimidated."
June Gregory

David

The trip to Reno made life easier for a time. I felt emotionally lighter, as if a heavy weight had been lifted. The usual difficulties, such as living in a strained marriage and trying to gain self- confidence at work, seemed so much easier. The constant rejection I experienced while recruiting felt so much less intense, and my results were remarkably improved. I began to realize that because I felt better, the people on the other end of the phone were more interested in hearing what I had to say. I had always assumed good recruiting was based on my ability to say the right thing at the right time. Now I saw a whole new reality. People were responding more to what I felt than what I said. The happier I was on the phone, the more interested they were no matter how well I said it.

My improved sense of well-being also made each call more fun and interactive. Without even trying, I was recruiting candidates left and right. The more candidates I was able to attract, the more fun I was having. The more fun I was having, the more candidates I was able to recruit. I was on a roll!

June and I were in sync as well. We would meet in the morning where she would tell me what kind of candidate she needed to recruit that day and then I'd go get them. At the end of the day we would meet again to go over my results. I was beginning to get a sense of what it was like to work in a team. Even though it was just the two of us, I was feeling the synergy that comes from working well together.

Everything in my life was vastly improved, all from what had seemed to be an innocent little trip to Reno. A trip I had originally fought tooth and nail not to go on. What had I been thinking? How could I have been so unaware of how completely out of whack my life had become. How could I have grown so accustomed to being unhappy? What if I had not listened to June?

All these questions led me to the same conclusion: I needed to learn to trust June more. It seemed I was coming to this same conclusion more and more these days, yet my execution left a lot to be desired. Somehow, the crazier June's ideas sounded to me, the more I ended up benefiting from them. Even if I didn't trust her, I needed to learn how to do whatever she suggested without putting up an argument, I told myself. I was always vacillating between two extremes. I either believed June was a phony who was truly out to destroy me. Or at times like this, I realized she was helping me to get free from the negativity that gripped me.

June continued to invite me to sit in on her interviews. "Eventually, you are going to need to learn how to do this," she told me. As I continued to witness these character dissections, I began to relax and appreciate what she was accomplishing.

June, I noticed, started out each interview by welcoming candidates and talking to them about something that had nothing to do with their job search. With women, she would usually compliment them on a piece of jewelry or article of clothing. Since June loved jewelry, she could spend 10 or 15 minutes (or longer!) exchanging details about rings, bracelets, earrings, etc. I would sit there uncomfortably wondering when the candidates were going to get upset with all her personal questions. But they never did.

Occasionally, June would ask me what I thought of a particular piece of jewelry. "Isn't that stunning?" she would ask. I would put on my best fake smile and say, "Yes, it's very nice." But all I was thinking was: Why are we wasting our time talking about jewelry?

With men, June would talk about watches, clothes or their hobbies. This was not some interviewing technique she had. She was genuinely fascinated by each and every person who came into the office. And the more I observed June's interviewing style, I began to notice I could tell a lot about people by the manner in which they responded to her overtures. Positive candidates became openly more friendly and outgoing. While the candidates who had attitude problems became more clearly defensive and mistrusting. Most candidates responded in one way or another to June's weight. Again, I noticed the more positive the candidate's attitude, the less they responded negatively to June's size. I was beginning to understand a lot was going on in those initial minutes of the interview.

Finally, after greeting and getting to know the candidate, June turned to the business of going through the application and résumé. She was meticulous about each line of the application, but there were four particular parts of the application she really focused on: 1) ideally, what they wanted in their next job; 2) the reason(s) for leaving each company they had worked for; 3) the reason(s) for accepting each new position; 4) their current salary and the salary they were now seeking.

June listened carefully as the candidates answered her questions. She wrote down notes on the application as they spoke. I began to realize she was listening for any inconsistencies in the candidate's story: for example, if a candidate said he left a position to reduce his hours but ended up working just as many hours in his new job. Or if a candidate felt her current company was underpaying her and she said she wanted the next company to pay her more than she knew she was really worth. June was like a detective trying to solve a case.

By focusing on these four questions, June was able to solve the mystery of each candidate's career with remarkable accuracy. Each candidate had a career story with a beginning ("I started my career wanting to be a…"), a middle ("Somewhere along the way I ended up becoming…") and an end ("Things aren't what I had hoped …"). And every candidate had something go wrong somewhere in their story. Very few career stories, I discovered, were going well. In fact, even the stories that looked so good on a résumé were, more times than not, going tragically wrong. Compared to their dreams and wishes, the candidates' stories were rarely happy ones.

115

And there was June doing everything within her power to discover exactly where the story had gone wrong. What underlying lie about themselves or the work world had they accepted? Who had betrayed them? Who were they trying to please?

She was like a career priest. For some reason I still could not fully appreciate, candidates felt comfortable revealing things about themselves they had never admitted to anyone (especially themselves). These meetings would often morph into something that looked more like a confessional than an interview. Candidates felt comfortable telling June about career dreams they had long forgotten. Or about mistakes and bad decisions they made that they had been covering up for years.

And there I sat, totally uncomfortable, listening as candidates somehow found the courage to reveal their inner selves to June. I felt uneasy with their vulnerability, probably because I was still so uneasy with my own. I knew June had, so far, been amazing at helping me, but I was just beginning to fully appreciate how effective she could be in helping other people. And once she helped them understand their wounds, I watched as they became free to make better decisions – to live more fully.

By getting candidates to talk honestly about their regrets, wounds and poor decisions, June was freeing them from their limitations and allowing them to make career choices that met their true needs, wishes and goals.

It was during one particular interview with a sharp candidate named David that the full impact of what June was accomplishing hit me. The candidate was in sales. As June was going through his background, it became apparent that he had left three jobs in a span of six years for exactly the same reason. Each of the past companies he had worked for had promised him a promotion and increase in pay if he achieved his sales goals. In each case he had not only met those goals but exceeded them. And when it came time to collect his reward, each company had, according to the candidate, reneged on their original agreement.

The Interview

"Let me ask you something," June began. "Why do you think a smart, hard-working man with a great education, who could have his choice of companies to work for, keeps getting lied to by the management of his company?"

"Well, I wouldn't go so far as to say that they lied," he responded.

June sat up in her chair, "Really? What would you call it?"

"It's just the way it goes. I haven't found the right company yet, I suppose."

"Ideally, what are you looking for in a company?" she asked.

"A company I can grow with. I mean really grow."

"Isn't that what you were looking for the last three times? You keep striking out."

"I wouldn't call it striking out. That's unfair."

"What would you call it?"

"Things haven't worked out. That's all. That's why I'm here."

June adjusted herself again in her chair. "Let me get this straight. You have had three jobs in six years. Within those six years, you have never once experienced the growth you are telling me is your primary goal. And all you have to say for yourself is things just haven't worked out? The way I see it, you either have no desire to grow or you just enjoy being lied to and manipulated by others. Which one do you think it is?"

"That's ridiculous!" he shot back. "You are making far too big a deal out of this. I'm just here to find a new job. Can you help me or not?"

"I can't help you if you are not willing to look at yourself as part of the problem." I could feel June's strength begin to fill the room, a feeling I was becoming very familiar with. "Look, you keep being told one thing when you are hired and then experience another when you have delivered on your end of the bargain. You have been lied to and manipulated in every job you've had over the last six years. I asked you what you wanted ideally in your next career move and all you can come up with is the exact same goal and priority you've been focused on throughout those six years. Nothing in you has changed or seems to want to change. Despite all the frustration, lack of growth and changing jobs every two years, you haven't figured out one thing about yourself."

As was now my custom, I sat there feeling very uncomfortable. I looked at the candidate halfway expecting him to get up and leave the room or, worse, to jump over the desk and clobber June. But that's not what happened. He did the unexpected. He softened.

"What should I do," he asked.

"Your focus, your goal, has been on growth. The problem with each position hasn't been a lack of growth; it's been a lack of integrity."

I snuck a quick look at the candidate. He was looking at June differently now. I could see that he was really taking it all in.

"Your frustration and lack of growth is the result of not learning from your mistakes. The reason you left your first company was due to a lack of integrity in the leadership of the company. They said one thing and then did the exact opposite. The next company did the same thing and the next. Each time you are lied to and manipulated, you respond by wanting more growth which only makes it all that much easier for you to be manipulated by the next company."

"I hadn't looked at it that way" he said.

"You say you want growth when what you desperately need is integrity. You need to learn how to identify and ask for what you really want. Learn that and I would be willing to bet a man like you will find more growth than he ever thought possible."

June was looking him straight in the eyes. When I looked over at him, this well-dressed, successful-looking man began to get teary-eyed.

"You are right. I don't know why I couldn't see it. I keep picking companies that lack integrity. They tell me what I want to hear and I believe them. I guess I've wanted to find a company where I could grow so badly that I don't really pay proper attention to what kind of people they really are," he said.

"That's right," June responded.

"You know the funny part of all this? When I think back on my interviews with each of the past three jobs, I had a feeling in my gut that something wasn't quite right. But then when they would start talking about the possible growth, I would get excited and stop paying attention to that feeling. It's strange."

"In this case, that feeling was your instincts trying to tell you this job was not the right one for you. But you didn't listen, so you had to learn the hard way. I have a saying, 'Show me someone who wants to learn, and I'll show you an amateur!'" June said laughing.

"You are right! You know once I ignore that instinct I just forget I ever had it in the first place. Instead of blaming myself for picking the job, I end up getting mad at the management," he confided.

Now it was my turn to be impressed. He went from defensive to humble and open in a matter of minutes. Why couldn't I do that? I envied him a little.

"You are starting to figure it out. Good for you," June told him.

"I must say that I never had anything like this happen to me in an interview before. In fact, nothing like this has ever happened to me! No one has challenged me like this," he said.

"You are smart, hard-working, and I love that you are such a go-getter. We need to find you a company with great leadership. A company with integrity, fairness and the desire to grow," June concluded.

"You know it's interesting that you keep pointing out the issue of integrity. When I was a kid my dad rarely talked about his work. The few times he did say something it was to complain about how the company he worked for never kept their promises to him. He would complain, but he would never do anything about it. He worked for the same aerospace company his whole career. I can remember telling myself that I wasn't going to make the same mistake he did. I promised myself if a company ever lied to me I would leave," he said.

"Well, you kept your promise to yourself, but do you see how you are repeating exactly what your father did?" June replied.

"I'm not sure I'm following you."

"You are not afraid to walk away like he was, but you keep putting yourself in the exact same position as he was in. You keep choosing different companies that make promises they don't keep. He picked one company that did the exact same thing. You tell me, what's the difference? If you don't change your approach to your career you are going to get to the end of your life having never experienced what it was like to work for leadership you respected and admired. Who does that sound like?"

"Well at least I would be able to say that I kept trying. That's got to count for something doesn't it?"

"No, that doesn't count for anything at all! You tell me which man is better off: the man who stays his entire career in a job where he allows himself to be manipulated or the man who changes jobs every two years and consistently chooses to work for companies that manipulate him? Who is better off?" she pressed.

There was a long pause. I continued to sit there. I was back to feeling completely uncomfortable, even shrinking in my seat a little. I felt like I was the audience at someone's therapy session or, worse, their hanging.

"Yeah, you're right. It doesn't sound any better, does it? Man, June, this is tough. Here I was telling myself I was doing the exact opposite of what my dad had done with his career when, in reality, I've been doing the exact same thing. I've been blowing it."

He sat there no longer looking like the confident, even cocky, successful salesman who had walked into our office. Instead he looked more like a little boy who had just been told that he couldn't have the new bike he so desperately wanted.

"I don't know if I can change," he said looking down at his chair.

"That's ridiculous. Are you going to give up on yourself just because you've made some mistakes? Maybe you're not the go-getter I thought you were." Again June was pressing him.

"Well, how do I change this? I don't even know if there are companies that have the kind of integrity you are talking about."

"Would you say that you are being treated with integrity right now?" she asked him.

"What do you mean?"

"Right now, this very minute, do you feel you are being treated honestly and respectfully?"

"Yeah, most headhunters just find out what you want and then send you out to the job they want you to have whether it is a fit for you or not. They are just out for their fee. No, you are definitely different. You seem to really care," he answered.

"Well, there you have it. Since you are presently sitting in a company that has integrity, then there must be other companies out there that have it. Wouldn't you say?"

"Okay, but I know there can't be too many companies where the leadership really cares, especially when it comes to sales. Everybody is always just trying to make more money. They're always about more money and more growth."

"That sounds a lot like you – money and growth," June replied sternly, in a tone that I thought only I was capable of bringing out in her. "Listen, you said that you were not sure if you could change. The real question is: do you really want to change? The reason you are so unsure of your ability to change is not because you're not sure that you can. You feel that way because you're not sure you want to."

"Do you really believe that, June?"

"Yes I do. A man like you could do anything he set his mind to, including finding leadership he respected. You said it yourself. You told me that you had a bad feeling about every job you took, but you chose not to pay attention to it. Now imagine you not only started paying attention to those instincts, but you also got very clear on what you really wanted in the first place."

"You mean focus on looking for a company where the leadership has integrity?"

"I hope that's what I mean since that's what we've been talking about here for the past half hour. You know, I have to say for someone who appears to be so smart, you really can act pretty dumb," she said.

Sitting there, I thought: *There, she did it again! She insulted him right in the middle of giving him constructive criticism. And he was really coming around. He was being so honest with her. Come on, the poor guy was in tears! Why does she always have to do that? Why does she have to always push like that? He's definitely not going to stand for that. He's going to get up and leave or worse!*

"Yeah, I guess from your perspective it must look that way. I'm really sorry; I'm not trying to be difficult. It's just this is all new to me," he said.

Somehow she got away with it again, I thought. *Not only is he not angry, he's apologizing.*

"I understand this is new, but if you don't start learning how to be honest with yourself, you will never have what you really want," June said.

"I thought I was being honest with myself, but I'm beginning to see by not listening to my instincts I was compromising. I would love to work for a company where I trusted and respected the leadership. I really would," David told her.

"Do you believe they are out there?" June asked.

"Yeah, I do. When I think about it I had two or three clients over the years that had the qualities in their leadership you are talking about. Everyone I met working there seemed so happy and energized. I even remember thinking to myself I should go to work for them but, for some reason, I never followed up on it."

"You've got to want good leadership more than you want growth if you are ever going to work for a company with integrity. You will never grow until you learn how to make that change," June said.

"It's funny, I always thought about growth in terms of becoming a vice-president and making more money. But what I'm getting is my growth is really about me becoming who I want to become. It's not a title or a salary I want. It's really an experience I'm after. I want to grow as a person. I don't want to end up like my dad – totally burnt out and unhappy. I want to feel alive and excited about my job. Who cares what they call me? And as long as I can afford to live, I really don't care how much I make. That's it. I really want to grow, but I want to grow toward something more fulfilling."

He was sitting up straight in his chair. David was very excited about what he had realized about himself.

"The way you can achieve what you are after is to seek out leaders that already have it. That's the fast track to learning anything. If you can find people who have learned how to find meaningful success in their careers, you can learn from them," June said.

"Those are leaders who have integrity?" he asked.

"Yes, that's the most important thing to focus on in your search. But they also need to have good business sense and a position where you can use as much of your experience, skills and education as possible," June said.

"That makes a lot of sense."

"Good! I'm glad we are finally communicating!"

"What if I find a company with great leadership, but the job isn't quite right? What should I do in that case?"

"What do you think you should do?"

"Well, I know that there aren't that many companies out there with great people running them. Believe me, I deal with a lot of companies, I can honestly say I've only seen the two or three that I mentioned. So I guess if I do find one, I need to be open. Is that right?" he asked.

"Yes, that is exactly right. The opportunity to work for a company like that is going to be a once or twice in a lifetime deal. And that's if you're very lucky!"

"Okay, so I know I will need to be flexible. I'm willing to do that, if that's what it takes."

"Good for you. Here's a good way of thinking about your job search. Get clear on the positive feeling you want to experience working for your ideal company. On a scale of 0 to 10, the best feeling is a 10 and the worst is a 0. Take a moment and get very clear on what a 10 would feel like. You can borrow from the past or go to your dreams about your future, but stay away from the experience you are having in your current company. Let me know when you think you have it."

David took about 30 seconds then proclaimed, "Ok, I have it. That's a great feeling."

"Now pick a number on your ideal experience scale that you cannot and do not wish to go below. For example, tell yourself 'I will not work for any company below an 8 on my scale. I will be as flexible on EVERYTHING else as I can, but I will not work for a company that is less than an 8.' Make that promise to yourself and keep it. You can take temporary jobs or anything else you need to do to get by, but commit to not compromising."

"How do you know what number a company is by just an interview or two?"

"If you are clear on your number 10 experience and you commit to putting the quality of leadership as your first priority, trust me, you will know."

"I'll try it."

"You don't have to wait for your next interview to try it. When you go into a store or restaurant, you can give it a number. When you meet someone new, give them a number. The point is not to become judgmental. The purpose is to exercise your ability to hear your instincts so you can begin to act on them," June explained. "When your mental focus is on track and you are listening to your intuition, you are in the best position to discern great opportunities from poor ones. You've got to have both. The right focus without being intuitive or being intuitive without the right focus will not get you the results you want."

"You're really talking about how to make a good decision. That's been my problem. I don't know how to make a good decision," he confessed.

"Yes, a great career is based on the ability to make great decisions. That's true. But in order to have the right focus in your career you have to learn how to understand yourself and you have to learn how to give to yourself, how to love yourself. Without that, 'growth' doesn't really mean anything," June said.

I was totally enthralled by June's conversation with the candidate. She was so impressive. But I felt uncomfortable (again) with this idea of "love yourself" in a job interview. It seemed out of place to me.

"I'm not sure what you mean by learning to love myself. How does that show up in my work life?" David said. I was so glad he said it and not me.

"It's everything! Your dream of career growth comes down to a simple question: Are you going to decide to give yourself what your dad could not? You said he didn't give you what you really wanted. The question is: Are you going to learn how to give yourself what you need, or are you going to end up an unhappy martyr like him?" she asked.

"That's loving myself – if I give myself what I really want in my work life?" he asked.

"Can you think of a more intimate, important, more touching gift than giving yourself what you have always desired in your career?" she asked.

David paused. Then he said, "Well, a beautiful, loving woman wouldn't hurt!"

The three of us had a good laugh. I could have hugged the guy for bringing some humor to my constant discomfort.

June said, "I said *career*! Besides what would an amazing woman like that be doing with a martyr like you?"

Still laughing, he said, "You're right! I better clean up my act fast if I want a good woman. But to be honest with you, June, I really can't think of a more important thing I could do to improve my life than go after the work experience I've always dreamed of. I mean even if I never find it, at least I'll know I have given it my all. Just that thought alone has me feeling better about myself and my life than I have in a long time."

"That's how you learn to love yourself. That's how you learn to give to yourself. That's what will bring you the fulfillment you are looking for. When you learn to love and give to yourself, you will naturally want to give to others. That's where the fulfillment comes in."

"It's just that simple?"

"No, you have to work hard for this kind of life. That's why so few people have it. No one is going to just come along and give this to you. You are going to be tested over and over again. You'll see opportunities that seem right but aren't. You might lose faith you will find great leadership to work for. You may even find the right leadership but be tested through your own misperceptions brought on by your own mistrust," she said.

I quickly realized June's last comment described my situation perfectly. I was in the right situation, but I was being haunted by the wounds and ghosts of my past. I was consistently living under the assumption I would be betrayed by June, just as my mom and dad had betrayed me during my youth. Every unexpected turn felt like a possible land mine. I was trying so hard to trust her, but no matter how hard I tried, my past wounds would raise their ugly heads. I was learning if I was ever to recover from the pain and difficulties of my past, I was going to have to learn how to trust again. Not just trust – but trust the right person. And clearly June was that person. In my case, the only chance I had for success was to learn how to mistrust my feelings of mistrust. As I sat there, I knew exactly what I needed to do to experience my dreams of growth and success.

"The most difficult aspect of this will be to hold onto your expectation of fulfillment," June added, "to continue to believe you will have your 8, 9 or 10. That's why it's so important to minimize your exposure to negative people. People who bring you down are absolutely lethal to finding true growth and success. Of course, once you are firmly rooted in a great environment, then you can reach out and try to help those same folks. But until you find what you're looking for, avoid them as much as possible."

"Yeah, my brother is that person. Every time I'm around him, I find myself down. He has his own very successful company, but the guy is constantly stressed out. He's the unhappiest person I know. He is always telling me to quit my job and look for something that pays more. But it wouldn't matter how much money I made, he would always think I should be making more. That's just how he sees the world. Another friend of mine that I went to school with thinks I should just give up on the whole work thing, as he calls it, and go off hiking and traveling the world. But that guy is as unhappy as my brother! He never works, he is always borrowing money and he's a downer. The more I think about it, I really need to stay away from both those guys."

As David said that, I could see him coming back to life. He looked different physically. His eyes were bright, his body more relaxed and his overall demeanor was strong and at peace.

June finished the interview, and he thanked her, "As I said, June, I've never had a conversation like this. I can't tell you how much I appreciate what you have done for me. I promise you that I will not forget it, and I will make you proud."

June stood up to shake his hand, but she wasn't quite finished. "Don't be afraid to try for what you want. It's better to fail at that than to succeed at compromise. Your fear is you will find out what you really want doesn't exist. But keep trying. When it comes to integrity, growth and listening to your instincts, always keep trying. Focus on integrity, let go of everything else. Decide you want to change. Decide you want better. Decide to learn from your father's mistakes. Don't repeat them. That's your mission. Fulfilling that mission will make you happy and your Dad proud of you even if he could never admit it."

About a month after their initial interview, June placed David with one of her clients. The day he accepted the position, he sent June a card and a dozen red roses. The card read: "I found my 10 and I feel like a new man! To celebrate, I'm taking my dad to his favorite restaurant. June, how can I ever repay you?" - David

"I can't help you if you are not willing to look at yourself as part of the problem."
June Gregory

Brian

As I moved into my fourth month on the job, I began to become aware of another problem. Because of my complete and total lack of business experience, I had absolutely no understanding of most of the positions I was recruiting for. I would be recruiting for an accounting manager without any comprehension of what an accounting manager did for a living. Even if I was lucky enough to engage a potential candidate on the phone, they would very quickly figure out that I had no clue what I was talking about. Trying to convince a stranger to consider a career change when you sound like a complete idiot was not, as you might imagine, a formula for success.

Nevertheless, not knowing what else to do with me, June had me recruiting for a sales representative for one of her clients. After a week of calling hundreds of companies (the positive effects of Reno had worn off by now – each cold call was agonizing for me), I finally managed to recruit my first sales candidate. I was so happy with myself! My candidate came in to interview with June, and she spent time talking with him. I was anxious to have June like him.

After going over his background, she observed that he had a tendency to avoid risk in his career. She asked him why he felt the need to play it safe. I don't remember what he said. I do remember June ended the interview very quickly. Then June very calmly asked me what I thought of him. I was excited. I told her that I thought he was great. He had stayed at his jobs for a long time and seemed like a really nice guy. She listened and then said these six words, "He's not sharp enough. Keep recruiting."

I was beside myself. How could she just dismiss a good guy like that? How could she come to such a quick decision about him? Obviously,

I thought to myself, June didn't realize I had called almost every sales organization in the area and this was the only guy interested in our client's position. He had a good background, he was friendly and stable. June was being too hard on him.

I told June how I felt and she very patiently tried to explain to me the qualities of a place able sales representative. She pointed out my candidate always did just enough to get by, but he had never truly excelled at any of his jobs. She also pointed out while he had been stable, he also chose companies to work for that lacked strong management. "He doesn't think he has what it takes to be successful, so he plays it safe. He doesn't believe in himself and when I tried to talk to him about that quality, he didn't want to get into it. Until he is open to talking about that fear, he is not going to be the quality of candidate that we place."

I listened to June's explanation, but all I could think of was how hard I had worked to recruit this candidate. I felt, despite what she was saying, I had earned some kind of success. June quickly observed that I wasn't paying attention to her and changed tactics. "I can see that you are not listening to a word I'm telling you. Since you think he is a good candidate, why don't you get on the phones and market him? You find him a job."

That was exactly what I wanted June to say. This was my chance to prove myself and to prove June wrong. In sports and in school, I had always performed best when other people said that I couldn't reach a goal. Under a good challenge, I had almost always proved doubters wrong. With a new-found motivation and sense of purpose, I got on the phones and started marketing my candidate. I called everyone. Because I was talking about a real person and a job I had some understanding of, I had a sense of confidence I had not had in any of my previous cold calling. I was clear and determined. I made hundreds of calls. I spoke to sales manager after sales manager after sales manager.

After two weeks of marketing, I did not have a single interview for my candidate. No one, not even companies that needed sales representatives were impressed with his résumé. Eventually, it hit me I had been defeated.

June had watched me during this time without saying a word. Then I realized there were simply no more companies to call. With my tail between my legs, I went into her office and admitted I had been wrong. June didn't say much, but later that day she invited me back into her office.

When I got there I found June and a very professional, well-dressed and obviously very confident man. "Brian, I'd like you to met Jim, a sales representative I have placed in his last two positions." The moment I saw him, I got the point. This guy was impressive. He stood up, looked me right in the eyes and, with a big smile, shook my hand. As he spoke I saw he was extremely professional, very positive, really enjoyed his work and appeared fearless. He was the picture of success. Comparatively, he made my candidate look tired, unmotivated, and unpolished.

Jim told June that after five years he felt that he had grown as much as he could with his current company. He loved the company June had placed him in but felt if he was going to continue to grow he needed a company where he would be exposed to new challenges. I just sat there and listened to the two of them talk. June was so proud of his growth. He was so appreciative of what June had done for him. "Without her," he told me, "I would probably still be working in that retail store for that crazy boss."

Within a week June had arranged three interviews for Jim, and he accepted what he called "an opportunity of a lifetime" with one of June's clients – a local high tech company. I had another taste of humble pie. This job wasn't like sports or school. This challenge was on a whole new level. It wasn't enough to deal with the constant fear of rejection while making cold calls, I had to learn how to recruit candidates like Jim. I had to learn how to recruit exceptional candidates. As Jim and June sat in her office laughing and enjoying the victory of Jim's new opportunity, I realized how much I had to learn and how far I had to go. Even though I didn't understand the difference between an accounts payable clerk and an administrative assistant, I was going to have to figure out the difference between an exceptional candidate and an average one.

On the long drive home that evening I began to feel very discouraged. The fact I had just spent two weeks marketing the wrong candidate was bad enough. The fact I didn't even know what an exceptional candidate was – now that's overwhelming. Then I had an epiphany.

It occurred to me the reason I didn't understand what made for an exceptional candidate was because I wasn't one myself. I was not an exceptional candidate on any level. In fact, I was a worse, much worse, candidate than the nice guy I had just spent so much time marketing. And compared to Jim, well I didn't even want to think how I compared to him. I was quickly coming to the realization I was at the very bottom of the pack. I was insecure, dressed unprofessionally and didn't have much, if any, confidence. I didn't understand business. I didn't understand people. I didn't, as June was constantly pointing out, understand the first thing about myself. And with my "I'll show you" attitude toward June, I had not only proved she was right about my negatives, I had somehow managed to show her I was stubborn too. On that long ride home, I saw myself as I really was and I didn't like it.

The only positive I was able to discover on that extra-long ride home was I had taken the job so that I could get at the truth about myself. And the truth, as ugly as it seemed to me at that moment, was exactly what I was getting. If June could do as much for Jim as he had claimed, surely she could help me too. June had, for reasons I could not understand, hired me. Maybe I was at the bottom of the candidate pool, but she had selected me. That was my one saving grace. That was something to hold on to.

When I arrived home, my pursuit of the truth came face to face with another reality: money. My two-week venture to place my candidate and prove myself right had resulted in no placements and no commissions. My 100% commission job was paying me 100% of nothing and I was at my wit's end. No money meant no rent, no food, and no gas. The money we had been living on – money given to us by Robin's family – was about to run out.

Because of the positive effects working for June had on me, I had done everything in my power not to think about my money problems. Had

God really answered my prayer as I had thought He had? Somehow I just couldn't imagine a God that would want me to fail when I was doing what I thought was the right thing. But when faced with the reality of the situation, I was beginning to believe that God could allow such a thing to happen. Maybe He was hard, uncaring and mean. My thoughts and emotions vacillated back and forth between hope and faith and darkness and despair. I was tortured.

The next day at work, it became clear to me that realistically I needed at least three more months before I would learn enough to make a placement. I had a week's worth of money left and a wife and baby to house and feed. This job was the most difficult undertaking I had ever taken and despite my ability to do well in school and in sports, I had met my match. I had lost. I decided to tell June I had to quit. When I went to tell her of my decision, she was tied up in interviews, so I left for home and resolved to come back in the morning and hand her my resignation.

On the way home, I was imaging how I was going to break the news to June and what her reaction would be. I was deep in thought waiting for a traffic signal to change, when suddenly I felt a hard jolt. Someone had slammed into the back of my – already beaten up – car. The driver got out and nervously explained he was not paying attention and that he didn't want the accident reported to his insurance company. He offered me cash. I got out of my car, surveyed the damage – a small dent – and followed the man to his bank.

When I got home, I discovered that after paying all the bills, rent, food and gas, the money received from the accident would allow me to continue to work for June for exactly three more months. To the penny.

"People who bring you down are absolutely lethal to finding true growth and success."
June Gregory

Jennifer's Prep Session

How to Interview with Confidence

The day finally arrived for Jennifer, the Stanford graduate who didn't know what she wanted to be when she grew up, to go on her interview with the venture capital firm. Before June would send a candidate out for an interview, she always had them come into her office to prepare them. I soon learned that these prep sessions were every bit as life-changing as the interviews. June had a remarkable way of bringing out the very best in a person before they went out for the interview. The prep or send out, as she called it, for Jennifer was one of the first I got to sit in on. "I want you to watch and learn how to do this. Someday you will need to be doing this on your own," June told me.

Jennifer came to the send out dressed in another great suit. The two of them talked while I sat there in my typical pensive manner waiting for the "real" send out to begin. Finally after what seemed like a long time (but was actually less than five minutes), June got down to business.

"Are you excited about the interview?" June asked.

"Well, yes. But I need to meet them first to see whether I like it or not," she replied.

"Really? Let me ask you a question. What if it turns out to be the best opportunity of your life?"

"Then, of course, I will be excited," she said.

"At what point in the interview will you show your excitement?"

"I don't know. When I understand what a good opportunity it is, I guess," she said sounding confused.

"And what level of enthusiasm will you express up until that moment?"

"I don't know. I guess my average level."

"Now let me ask you an important question: what level of excitement do you think a company that has the best opportunity of a lifetime will be looking for?"

"I'm not sure I understand your question."

"Let's say you are interviewing at the best company you could ever imagine. What would they be looking for in terms of a candidate's attitude and enthusiasm?"

"I guess they would be looking for someone who was really positive and excited to work there."

"Back to your approach to interviewing, you said you would be excited only after you knew you were right for the opportunity. How do you imagine a company like the one I just described would view your attitude, motivation and level of enthusiasm during the period BEFORE you figured out how fantastic they were?"

The lights went on. "That's a good question. They wouldn't like it. They would probably see me as lacking enthusiasm for the position."

"That's right. Let's say you have one ticket for a very special event, and you have two friends you are trying to choose between to take with you. You call friend #1 and ask her if she would like to join you. She responds by asking you to describe the event. She wants to know the particulars. You oblige and when she hears the details, she is extremely excited. You then call friend #2 and ask her the same question. Friend #2 says she would love to join you. She is excited to go to the event with you before she has even heard the particulars. Who are you going to invite?"

"Of course, the second friend!" Jennifer responded.

"Why is that?" June asked.

"She was excited about going with me not just about a free ticket to a great show."

"That's right. Now let me ask you. Since you have decided to offer the ticket to friend # 2, does friend # 2 have to accept once you fill her in on the details of the event?"

"No, I suppose not," she answered.

"And who are you more likely to give more details about the event to?" June asked.

"Friend #2 because her attitude wasn't conditional like the first friend's," Jennifer said.

"Now are you getting my point?"

"Yes, that's amazing. By being more positive and enthusiastic, the second person gets the offer," replied the now-enlightened candidate.

"Yes, and more information as well. This is the first rule of good interviewing. There is nothing to think about, worry about or analyze UNTIL YOU HAVE AN OFFER. Great interviewers understand this simple point of logic and bring their highest hopes and expectations to the interview. They bring a genuine enthusiasm – just in case the interview turns out to be the opportunity of a lifetime," June said.

"That changes everything, doesn't it?" Jennifer asked.

"Yes it does. It means you have to learn to leave your fears and concerns at the door before you interview."

"How do I do that?"

"The first step is to identify what your fears and concerns actually are. Do you know what they are?" June asked.

"Well, since I'm not really sure what I want to do with my career, my first fear is I'll decide to accept a position and then discover I don't really want to do it," she said sheepishly.

June sat up straight. "Well, given that concern, maybe we should cancel the interview, so you don't have to worry about making that mistake."

Jennifer interrupted June, "No, I want to go. I am really looking forward to this!"

"We talked about this exact point for over half an hour. For such a smart young woman, you sure can be dense. If you are going to focus on the type of position as your first priority, I can't work with you. You wouldn't know the right position if it walked up and hit you over the head," June said with exasperation.

I had to admit I got a secret satisfaction out of seeing other people blow it with June in the same manner I was always doing. But in this case, my pleasure was short-lived. I realized that I needed Jennifer to get on track in order for me to place her. For the first time, I spoke up without June having to encourage me.

"Not long ago I was exactly where you are," I offered. "I didn't know what I wanted to do. What June is trying to tell you is so important. It takes all the anxiety and fear out of this career discovery process. It's not what you do, it's who you do it for that really matters in your career," I said. I was feeling kind of proud of myself.

Now, to be honest, all the while I was saying this cool stuff to Jennifer I was thinking, "Please get what I'm saying so that we can place you in this position, and I can make some money." I hadn't grown that much.

I realized that, even though my motivations were selfish, the advice was crucial for her to understand if she was ever going to be happy in her work life. This was her chance to break free from fear and anxiety. It was a strange moment for me. My usual selfish side had just collided with my just beginning to blossom, best side.

"I'm really sorry, you guys. You are both right. I don't know why I keep slipping back into my old way of thinking. It's such a negative way of seeing things – it really is. I needed that pep talk. Thank you. I think my fear is I won't be able to handle the job, I'll fail," she said.

That was interesting. One moment Jennifer was acting as though she was too good for the job and the next moment she was admitting a fear of not being good enough and failing. I was seeing this pattern a lot. Candidates who acted as though they were above a particular position were actually afraid of it.

"Ok, that's helpful," June said. "So, let me ask you, when was the last time you actually failed at something?"

Jennifer thought about it, "I'm sure I have, but I can't think of anything right now."

"What if you gave your very best effort to a job but failed. Would you really feel that bad if you knew for certain that you had given it your best?" June asked.

"No, I guess I wouldn't."

"So let's look again at your fear of failing. You haven't failed at anything in recent memory and, having given it your best effort, you wouldn't feel too awful if you did blow it. Is that true?"

"I must seem pretty ridiculous to the two you."

"Not at all," June said. "You have to process in order to understand yourself better. It took me years to understand my fears and insecurities."

"And I'd trade you my fears for yours anytime you'd like," I added.

Jennifer laughed. "Okay, that really helps. I feel better. Who cares if I fail as long as I give it my best shot, right? Besides if I never try, if I live in fear my whole life, how will I ever know if I have what it takes to make it?" she asked.

"Great, that's it," June exclaimed. "Now you've got the second part of being a great interviewer: identify your fears and insecurities, and don't bring them with you on the interview. Let go of your fears and doubts. Then you become free to bring your best self – your true self – to the interview. You can never be yourself when you are feeling intimated. You must work to eliminate intimidation. You do that by finding your fear, then working to let it go until it no longer has any power over you. For example, my insecurities are around my weight. I was in show business for most of my life, so I used to look down at anyone who was just a little overweight. Now I look at myself and I can't believe it. I'm very ashamed of myself. But it doesn't do me any good to put myself down. So if I was interviewing for a job, I would make a deal with myself that I would not allow myself to feel insecure about my weight problem. I would keep that up for the entire interview. As soon as the interview was over I could go back to my insecurities but, during the interview, I would not give anyone the pleasure of seeing my fears."

"Wow, that's great. But how do you do that, June?"

I had to admit, I was curious too.

"I would start by asking myself: do I want to work for a company with leadership that would make a hiring decision based on whether or not a candidate was overweight," June said.

"I wouldn't want to work for a company like that," Jennifer said.

"Neither would I. So why should I worry about what a company I wouldn't want to work for thinks of me?" June said.

Again Jennifer laughed, "It's so obvious, it's almost ridiculous! You have such a great way of seeing things, June. Of course, you wouldn't want to work for that kind of company."

"Exactly, let's go back to your fear that you will fail. Would you want to work for a company that was so unforgiving that they would fire someone like yourself? Someone who gives her best to what she is learning?"

"Not when you put it that way, I wouldn't."

"In order to be yourself in this interview that's exactly how you will need to look at it," June explained.

"You know, it really is true. I wouldn't want to work for a company like that," Jennifer repeated.

I could see she got it. She sat up in her chair, pulled her shoulders back and suddenly had a look of confidence. I hadn't even realized how much her body language had been showing her intimidation. Now she was, as June put it, "free to be herself."

"Ok, we covered the importance of being positive and the importance of identifying and freeing yourself of your fears. There is one more skill to becoming an expert interviewer. You have to learn how to be focused," June said.

"How does that work?"

"When you go out to eat, do you prefer meat or fish?" June asked.

"I don't like fish, so I always get the meat or pasta," she said.

"Have you ever had a waiter tell you about the specials for the evening and he starts describing halibut or salmon? What do you do when that happens?" June asked.

"I tune out. I stop listening and my mind begins to wander."

"Does it make you feel closer to the waiter?"

"No, it makes me feel awkward because I have to pretend to be listening. I have to pretend to be nice when I'm not really paying attention," Jennifer explained.

"Now, conversely, have you ever been out to dinner and the waiter begins to tell you about the specials, and it's the exact food you were hoping to have that evening, prepared exactly the way you love to have it?" June asked.

"Not very often, but I have had that happen a couple of times," Jennifer said.

"How did that make you feel toward the waiter? Did you feel closer to him or more distant?"

"That's easy. I felt closer. In fact, the last time that happened I felt like the waiter was a kindred spirit. It felt like he really knew me. I loved that whole evening," she said.

"What you see in these examples is the importance of being focused versus being unfocused. The only difference between the two waiters was that the first one was talking about food you didn't want or like. The second waiter was talking about your favorite food. It's really no reflection on who they are as people. One was just lucky and got it right, and the other was unlucky and got it wrong. Yet, look at the effect the difference had on you. The first waiter is causing you discomfort because you have to fake being nice. The second waiter feels like a long-lost friend." June explained.

"Wow, you're right. That's an amazing difference. The truth is if I got to know both waiters, I might have liked the first one over the second," she said.

"That's right, but you probably will never have the chance to really get to know them, so all you have to go by is this one interaction. The great news about interviewing is you get to know what the company is looking for before the interview. Just think if the first waiter had stopped long enough to ask you if you had preferred to hear about the fish or meat specials. If he had asked that simple question, he wouldn't have lost you. That's the position you are in. You know what this company is looking for. Now the question is, are you going to use that information to get focused or are you going to be unfocused and tell them all about your fish specials?"

"Let me ask you, where did you get that beautiful necklace you are wearing?" June asked unexpectedly.

"My mom and dad bought it for me when I graduated Stanford. It means a lot to me. It's jade, which I absolutely love!" she said.

The question about jewelry made me very nervous. I was hoping that June wasn't going to regress just when we were making so much progress!

"What if your parents had given you a football instead?" June asked.

Jennifer laughed, "I wouldn't have liked it at all, especially compared to the necklace."

"Wouldn't you say that your parents got very focused on what to give you for a present?" June asked.

"Yes, I couldn't have been more touched," she replied.

"Let me ask you. Are you as focused on what the company you're interviewing with today needs?" June asked.

"When you put it that way, no, I'm not."

"Just like your parents, you've been told exactly what they are looking for. You know the skills they need most. You know the attitude and level of enthusiasm they are looking for. And you have everything they want. So are you going to bring them a football or jade? Are you going to go on and on about the fish or the meat?"

"That's a great point, June. I think I was so caught up in my own worries, to be honest; the only thing I was thinking about was what they could do for me. I didn't even stop to think what I could do for them. That's awful to admit, but it's true."

June and Jennifer spent the rest of the prep time getting motivated and focused by going through a mock interview. June threw some really tough questions at her. I remember June asking her: Aren't you overqualified for this job? What if we hire you and you fail? Aren't you wasting your degree by starting in the front office? What if we hired you and thirty days after starting you weren't sure this was the right job for you? Tell me about yourself?

June was asking the toughest possible questions – questions that went right to the core of Jennifer's insecurities and fears. She was also asking questions that challenged Jennifer on her ability to focus on the company's needs, rather than her own. "Worry about your needs after you get the offer," June kept reminding her. And Jennifer was proving to be an amazing student. As the mock interview went on, she continued to improve dramatically. She was becoming increasingly more relaxed and confident. I was really impressed with her and, of course, June as well. June, the miracle worker.

I couldn't help but wonder how many years it would have taken Jennifer to get over her fears without June's help. It was clear to me her fear of failure would have defined her career. She would have never felt she was in the right job. If she ever had stumbled into the right opportunity she would have either not recognized it, or blown the interview or taken the job and then, out of insecurity, failed. I was beginning to appreciate more how large a part fear played in leading people to careers that lacked passion, accomplishment and fulfillment.

I was also deepening my understanding of the power in what June did for people. Here was this short, overweight ex-torch singer working in a two-person employment agency transforming peoples' lives at a level I could have never before imagined. Who was this woman? Where did she learn so much about life and how to help others in such a profound way?

It had never occurred to me how important a skill it was to learn how to interview. I was beginning to grasp it was every bit as important a life skill as an education or past job experience. I was seeing how large a part being able to be comfortable in your own skin and being focused and positive played in deciding who got offers and who didn't. Clients were far more interested in candidates who were confident and enthusiastic in the interview than they were candidates who had a better education or background but lacked confidence and enthusiasm in the interview.

June was able to teach Jennifer how to go from being a below-average interviewer to an expert in less than forty minutes. Jennifer's degree from Stanford had taken her four years and thousands of dollars to obtain, not to mention all the hard work and dedication. Yet, if June hadn't taught her how to recognize what she really wanted in her career, how to overcome her fears and how to interview, she would have remained lost and dissatisfied in her work life. All this was true. But what really struck me was that Jennifer was one of the better candidates I had interviewed. If an exceptional candidate needed this much help to find a job that would bring her fulfillment, I couldn't begin to imagine how much everyone else needed what June was offering.

How did a guy like me end up working for a woman like this? I asked myself. This question kept popping up more and more as the days went by.

Given June's comment about me doing a send out on my own someday, I had been taking notes throughout the meeting with Jennifer. I wrote down several keys to being a great interviewer:

1) In an interview, there isn't anything to worry about or analyze unless you receive an offer. Don't put the cart before the horse by over-thinking the opportunity before you know what it is.

2) Be positive. Approach every interview as though it was going to be the opportunity of a lifetime. By being positive, you will never have regrets about not being enthusiastic enough. If it turns out your excitement results in an offer you don't want, turn down the job. Only by being your best are you really in control. Fear is never your friend in an interview.

3) Be yourself. Don't try to be something or someone you're not. To be yourself you have to work to identify your fears, doubts and insecurities. Then you have to work even harder to let them go. If you don't do this well, you will end up feeling either intimidated or overconfident.

4) Get focused. Think about or, better yet, find out what the company is really looking for in a candidate. What are their priorities? What experience, skill sets and attributes do they need most? What is on their wish list? Make sure your answers reflect an honest and focused response. Think about the company's needs more than your own.

After Jennifer left the office for her interview with our client, I reviewed my notes. I read them over and over again. I suppose I was hoping if I memorized each word, I would be able to handle a send out like June. About my fifth go around at trying to memorize my notes, it hit me. It wasn't so much what June had said to Jennifer that was so powerful. It was the way she interacted with her that had resulted in all the positive change I had witnessed. June was fully engaged. Yes, she had a lot of wisdom, and yes she did understand a lot about interviewing. She understood points about interviewing I had never heard before. But the truly amazing thing about the send out was how June could speak to Jennifer in a manner that challenged her to her very core. June was not only able to help Jennifer identify her deepest fears around her work life, but she was able to free her from those fears as well. That wasn't a technique June had learned. It was far more than that. What was that quality she had? The more I thought about it, the more I was coming to the conclusion that it was more than just being fully engaged. If I was going to learn how to do a send out like June some day, I needed to learn what that special quality was.

On the way home from work I was listening to my favorite music. Once I found a song I really enjoyed, I would play it over and over again. One of the advantages of driving alone was I could indulge in my one-song habit without irritating anyone else. It was during one of those moments of pure musical bliss it hit me what June's special quality was. It was love. She genuinely loved people. It was out of her love for complete strangers that she found that rare combination of outrageous courage and overwhelming compassion to say the difficult thing – the thing that would reveal their deepest fears in a manner that was constructive, not critical.

Was I going to have to learn how to love others in order someday to do a send out? I thought. Given my current inability to love others, that could take me 20 years to learn, maybe longer!

It also occurred to me the only reason June had hired me was due to her capacity to love others. It was the only explanation that made any sense. With that revelation, I turned off the music and made a commitment. I would learn how to do a send out – no matter what it took.

> "Focus on integrity, let go of everything else."
> June Gregory

Brian

A Critical Juncture

By divine intervention or just amazing good luck, I had been given a three-month financial window to continue to work for June. I told myself (again!) this time I would listen to June's advice no matter what she suggested. I was committed to being a new man. I was going to be more open. I was going to be flexible and teachable. (It was amazing what having some money in the bank did for my attitude and disposition.)

June had me marketing to new companies in the morning and recruiting candidates in the afternoon. My goal continued to be to make 100 calls a day and talk to a minimum of 30 people. Each morning I went through the excruciating effort of making that first call. I hated the idea of being rejected, especially when I already felt like such a failure to begin with. I would do anything I could to forego getting on the phone. Even though I had only two or three items on my desk, I repeatedly, and unnecessarily, organized my work space. I would go to the restroom, whether I needed to or not. I looked out the window. I stared at the phone, as if by staring at it the phone would magically ring on its own. I daydreamed. I did anything not to make the first call.

Eventually I had developed a routine of avoidance. I had my standard series of behaviors I was able to drag out for a good thirty minutes or more. Only after thoroughly going through my routine would I find myself left with no other choice than to pick up the phone and make that first call. I can only imagine what June was thinking as she sat there each morning watching me go through my neurotic ritual. But, to her credit, she never said a word. Like a baseball player needs his rituals before getting into the batter's box, she must have sensed I needed mine.

Once I got on the phone I was always amazed at how remarkably nice most people were. Even though I was calling – and often interrupting – complete strangers, people wanted to help me. This came as a revelation to me. Of course, I got the occasional hostile individual. Those calls always set me back. Still, the more calls I mustered the courage to make, the more I came to realize angry people were clearly the exception, not the rule. I found this to be a tremendous relief, and it confounded my belief that people generally had a dog-eat-dog mentality. My courage grew. My opinion of other people and the world began to change.

My confidence was growing as well. I was actually beginning to enjoy talking with strangers. I still had trouble making that first call. I still had my morning avoidance ritual. However, the cold calling was getting more comfortable. By the end of each day I would leave energized.

Sitting in on her interviews, I noticed that June loved listening to the candidates' stories of success, but she evaluated their character by how well they handled their weaknesses and bad decisions. For June, their ability to communicate openly about mistakes was the key to determining their character. "Anyone can say what they feel good about. That doesn't tell you anything about them," she told me. "How well they can take responsibility for their mistakes tells you everything."

She was also quick to offer up her own poor choices. I realized even though she was remarkably forthcoming about her faults, weaknesses and poor choices, she never sounded sorry or guilty about her shortcomings. In fact, she had a way of communicating her faults in a manner that sounded like she was not unhappy that they had occurred. As she had done with me, she told candidates the story of how she had come to put on so much weight. She told them how she had worked at a bad company. She even told them how she had picked the wrong husband three times. Her strength didn't stem from not having weakness or from not having made bad decisions. Her weight alone was a clear testimony to that. I was learning June's strength came from being open about her mistakes and learning from them. In truth, her mistakes were actually much bigger than most of the mistakes or weaknesses the candidates were dealing with.

But, for many of them, when it came time for them to talk about the bad decisions and mistakes they had made in their careers, they were not comfortable being open or vulnerable. I could see how defensive and insecure they became when asked the same pointed questions June had asked me. I began to see how hard these candidates were working to cover up their weaknesses. The harder they worked at covering up their mistakes and fears, the more obvious it became they really needed to talk to someone like June in order to resolve them.

Then there were the positive candidates. In their own way they were just as predictable as the negative candidates. They were consistently fascinated by June and her remarkable insights and observations. They were not only willing to be honest and vulnerable about their fears and mistakes, they were excited to be talking to someone who cared and wanted to help them grow. They told June things about themselves they admitted they had not told anyone before. They hung on to her every word of advice. Sometimes they cried while communicating a difficult story. Typically, at some point in the interview, they usually shared a tremendous laugh with her. The longer they talked to June the more it sounded to me like two old friends just enjoying being in each other's company. And by the time the interview was over, three things always took place: 1) They were clear on exactly what they wanted; 2) They were excited and passionate about their future; and 3) They were confident they were going to find the job they really wanted.

Then June would place them. Somehow she always found a way to find these candidates the job they dreamed of having. I was flabbergasted by the process. It seemed almost like magic. When a candidate was able to remain positive, open-minded and flexible in the face of June's questions and constructive criticism, she would find them a job they loved and brought out the best in them. There weren't a lot of these positive candidates, but June somehow found a way to place each and every one of them.

I was also amazed at the fact that no matter what the candidate's attitude was, she always tried to counsel each and every person who came into her office. Even when it was apparent she was not going to be able to place the candidate, she would always take the time to talk to them about goals, motivations, fears and decisions. In essence, she gave each candidate the same opportunity she had given me. Even with defensive, closed-minded candidates, June was a master at connecting their ability to be more honest with themselves with their desires for growth, money and, ultimately, career fulfillment.

I sat and listened to her as she was able to convince candidates the more honest and responsible they were about their choices, the greater would be their ability to attract those same qualities in the next company they chose to work for. She explained to them a great match in her eyes meant placing a positive individual with a company that had positive leadership. Integrity, honesty, openness, and good business skills were the qualities that defined positive leadership. When a positive candidate was placed in a positive company, everyone grew. And while no candidate was perfect, no company was perfect either. The key was integrity. Was the leadership of the company and the candidate being honest and open with one another? Only when both sides were being honest about each other's negatives and weaknesses could a good decision be made. "Everyone will tell you their pluses, but the key to the match is each side CHOOSES THE OTHER'S NEGATIVES," she said. Only under these circumstances could the chances of either side being betrayed be avoided. Betrayal, on either side, was the death sentence of the match. "Betrayal kills any business relationship," June would explain. Integrity was an absolute necessity to making a good decision in any career move.

The more interviews I sat in on, the more I began to observe another interesting facet to June's approach. To my amazement, I observed June knew more about what the candidates wanted in their careers than the candidates themselves. She knew at the core of their desires and dreams, they wanted growth and fulfillment. Since she already knew what they wanted, June saw it as her job – her mission – to tell them what they wanted and how to get it. She could sound arrogant but at the end of the day, who could argue with the fact they wanted to experience more growth and fulfillment in their career? Like me, they might want to argue about the means of arriving at these aims or whether they were even possible, but no one could argue with her assumption they wanted to grow and experience more joy in their work lives. June not only knew what candidates wanted, she knew exactly what they needed to change about themselves in order to attain it. So each candidate got a strong dose of June's truth and accountability medicine. Some loved it, some ignored it, a few openly resisted it, but everyone got their fair share of it.

This woman was like no one I had ever met. She was not like other humans. She was a force of nature. June wasn't so much placing candidates in jobs as she was lifting them up – bringing out the very best in them.

She accomplished this feat by challenging them at their very core. June read each candidate's résumé and application as a story of their true selves revealed. Not through words (which are easily manipulated) but through their choices and actions. Choices and actions told her the true story. And, because she focused on their choices and actions, the candidates had no place to hide.

Once June was successful in helping a candidate express themselves openly and honestly and accept responsibility for their choices, they became free to make good, or even great, decisions. Rather than hiding from themselves and others, they were now free, usually for the first time, to simply be themselves. They were also free to start working on their weaknesses. The ability to work on your weaknesses was the absolute key to growth, according to June. "You cannot grow by continuing to draw on your strengths and avoiding your weaknesses," she stated emphatically.

June explained the central theme of an exceptional career was the ability to make good decisions. I watched June teach her candidates how to make great decisions. She was giving them the opportunity to take control of their work lives. She was giving them the tools, the mindset they would require to find the job of their dreams.

Needless to say, the more I learned about June, the more I was overwhelmed by the opportunity I had been given to work with her. It was shocking she had, for some unknown reason, picked me to mentor. Me – an angry, confused, bottom-dweller – somehow found myself learning how to help people figure out their careers and their lives. The irony of the situation, and my good fortune, was not lost on me.

However there were other realities to consider. I had now been well over six months on the job and, despite June's help and my increased call activity, I had not made a placement. My financial resources from the car accident were coming to an end. As my bills began to pile up again, my good attitude and appreciation for the job began to diminish. As impressed as I was with June, I began to have serious doubts I had what it took to make it. After an especially difficult day, I found myself again thinking I had made a mistake taking a job that didn't have a salary I could count on. It was out of frustration and self pity I decided to call my father for advice.

As I described earlier, I was not close to my father. But driven by an overwhelming fear of not having money, I called to get his advice. Since moving out to go to college, I had spoken to him only three or four times a year. Our conversations were always very short and superficial. But as damaged as our relationship was, I had always seen him as someone who knew how to do well in business and how to make money. So I told my dad all about my new job. I told him about my amazing new boss and about how much I was learning. I also emphasized the fact that the job was a 100% commission and I had not made a placement. Subconsciously, I was looking for his sympathy and perhaps some help financially. What I got was his advice. It was simple and straightforward.

My father told me I was to go into June's office and tell her I had financial responsibilities and I required a fair base salary. If she did not agree, he told me I should get up out of the chair and walk off the job. Once June realized I was man enough to quit over the issue, he explained, she would agree to come up with the money I needed. "That's how it works in the business world. Promise me you'll do it," he said.

After hanging up, I felt confused and unsure of myself. On the one hand, maybe my father was right. Maybe I needed to be more forceful. If this is how the world really worked, then taking charge and being more assertive with June was the answer to my financial nightmare. At this point, anything that would lead to more money looked awfully good. "Besides," I reasoned, "my dad knows how to make money."

On the other hand, I just couldn't imagine my father's advice working on someone like June. I didn't know much about business and even less about making money, but it seemed to me she just didn't seem like the kind of person who would go for confrontation. The money – I needed the money. The more I thought about the money the more I started feeling that my dad's approach was the right one. The more I thought about my unpaid bills and not being able to pay my rent, the more I started to believe paying me on commission only wasn't fair. I decided to confront June the next morning.

I woke up the next day in a strange daze. As I got up and started getting ready for work I felt as though I was just going through the motions. I was like a character in one of those old movies who has been hypnotized to carry out some mission he has no conscious awareness of doing. I drove to work in a mental fog. When I arrived at the office, I asked June if we could talk. As I sat down in her office, it hit me. I was afraid. I was extremely afraid. A sick feeling started in my stomach and began to spread throughout my body. Sitting across from June that morning felt surreal. It seemed as though I was watching the whole scene from some outside vantage point; as though I wasn't really in my body. But I knew I was in my body because it hurt.

June quietly and attentively listened to my request for a base salary that would allow me to pay my bills and expenses. I was aware my voice was shaking slightly as I spoke to her, and I felt angry at myself for not being stronger. When I was finished, she reminded me of our original agreement. June then explained to me the fact that it was taking me longer to learn the job than most people was not, in her mind, the basis for asking for a raise. Then in a very nice manner, she looked me square in the eyes (my stomach began to hurt more) and said, "the fact that you don't make enough cold calls, know how to interview, market to clients, understand the positions you are recruiting for and require a lot of my time and energy is not the basis, in my mind or anyone else's with any common sense, for a raise. If anything, it is a good cause for dismissal."

My stomach was turning inside out as I listened to her. "A deal is a deal," she said. "I have not broken my deal with you and I have very little patience with anyone who wishes to break a deal with me. I suggest you go home and really think about what you are doing. Frankly, I don't know if I want to have you working for me."

I wanted to yell out to June I didn't want to leave. Working for her had been the best thing that had ever happened to me. I wanted to tell her I didn't care enough about the money to let it stop me from continuing to have the opportunity to learn and grow in this job. But I didn't say anything. As if out of my body, I watched as I got up and left June's office. I watched as I gathered my few things off my desk. I listened as I said goodbye to June. I watched as I walked out of the building. I saw the car door open. I saw my car drive off.

As I drove home, I felt increasingly sicker. I kept playing the scene of asking for a raise over and over in my mind. Had I been strong like my father wanted me to be or had I just been stupid? Why did June's reaction make so much sense when my father's suggestion had sounded like the right thing to do? How could they both be right? And why was I feeling so physically and emotionally awful? Was it that difficult for me to be strong, or had I just made a terrible mistake? For the life of me, I didn't know.

I was about two miles from home and still going back and forth in my mind when I decided to pull off the highway. I knew that the moment I arrived home, my time with June would be over. Everyone I knew had encouraged me to ask for a raise or quit. The minute I stepped into my house, my friends and family would start congratulating me for finally leaving my commissioned job with June. My father would be the first to call to tell me that he was proud of me for having the guts to walk out on June as he had suggested. My friends, who at the time were just as unhappy, insecure and poor as I was, would rejoice in my decision. As I sat there in my car on the side of the highway, just a few minutes from home, I knew this was my last opportunity to think about June and what she stood for.

I sat there for several minutes. Nothing was clear. My fear of being broke was real. My bills and rent were real. But June's help was real too. My growth and confidence were evidence of that. Confused and exasperated, I leaned back in my seat and shut my eyes.

As I closed my eyes, my thoughts came to a stop. I saw thousands of little black dots floating around in front of me. I had experienced this phenomena many times as a boy. It took place when I shut my eyes on a sunny day. As a young boy I would try and count as many of the little black dots as I could before they eventually would disappear into darkness. I never could count more than 20 or so before they would be gone, but I knew that there were thousands of them. And here they were again, thousands of tiny black dots in the darkness of my vision. Then something unusual happened. I heard a car pass by on the highway and, in the brightness of the day, its reflection must have hit my side view mirror. The intense reflection was so bright it penetrated the darkness of my closed eyes and caused one of the tiny black dots to shine very bright. It was just for an instant on the far left corner of my panorama of black dots, but it was unmistakable.

Then it hit me. *That's my choice*, I remember thinking. Money, my dad, friends, common sense, being responsible, being reasonable, being accepted, being liked, and thousands of other reasons are the black dots. June is the fleeting, single, small bright dot of light. And there, right before my closed eyes, was my choice: Do I choose volume or luminosity?

Does the sheer volume of thousands of black dots assure me of security and happiness? Did the fact there were so many of them mean they represented the right choice?

But the single bright dot was unique. There was something about it that was attractive and made me feel more alive. But why was it the only one and why did it disappear so fast? The dot of light did not feel safe. The volumes of black dots were not bright. Both choices had their pluses and minuses.

I had been sitting on the side of the road long enough. I told myself to make my choice. Out of the sheer agony and pressure I felt to make a difficult decision, I also made a promise to myself whatever choice I made, I would never look back. I was going to commit myself fully to my choice. I grew quiet for a brief moment with my eyes still closed, took a deep breath and made my decision.

The aftermath was it took enduring an intense, two-hour conversation about the negativity of a person who lacks integrity, commitment and trust, who doesn't know the value of hard work and taking responsibility for his actions, and who doesn't know the nature of what it means to be a positive person, to convince June to give me one more chance. "You will not be given a third chance. If I can't trust you, you are of absolutely no use to me. Is that clear?" she asked. I nodded sheepishly. "Now get back to work. You've been a real disruption," she said while glaring at me.

I had made my choice. There would be no going back. And despite the two-hour lecture on my lack of character, my stomach had returned to normal.

Carolyn

During my seventh month on the job, I came across an electronic distributor company who was looking for a human resource manager. I liked the office manager immediately. She was positive, open and had worked with a search firm in the past. I spoke to June about the search then got busy recruiting for the position.

Being excited about the company helped me in recruiting. After a half hour or so making calls, I spoke to a woman named Carolyn who had a great personality on the phone and who was interested in hearing more about the position. She sent me her résumé and her background was a good match, so I set her up to interview with June.

Carolyn and June hit it off immediately. They talked about everything under the sun (except work!) for a good half hour. As was now our custom, June saw I was anxious for her to get started with the real interview but completely ignored me. During these personal interactions, I would always start to obsess silently: "June's using up all the candidate's time. 'He's going to have to leave before we can interview him,' or 'She's not going to think we are professional enough,' or 'I could be marketing or recruiting instead of wasting my time listening to these two.' I was always worrying. Meanwhile, June didn't seem to have a care in the world. We made for a strange study in contrasts.

June went through Carolyn's application, and then asked her to tell her about her current position.

"I used to love my job," she began. "I started out as an assistant to the HR manager. Then when that person left the company I was promoted into that position. I loved being involved in the hiring process and employee relations."

"What happened? Why are you looking for a new position?" June asked.

"Well, basically, my boss doesn't have a backbone. We have a few disgruntled employees who have awful attitudes toward their work and the company overall. My boss asked me to deal with them. I spoke with them and asked them to tell me what they were unhappy about. I also asked them what the company could do to remedy their problems. I was able to help them with a few of their complaints, but in a very short period of time they were complaining about more issues," she explained.

"What did you do next?"

"I went to my manager and explained to him what was going on. I told him, in my opinion; I felt that no matter what I did for the two employees, they were going to continue to be unhappy. They just felt entitled to having everything their way. There was no middle ground to meet them on. I also told him their attitudes were affecting the rest of the staff. These two sour grapes were managing to bring down the overall morale of the company."

"Well, you certainly explained that well."

"Thank you! I thought so, but now I'm not so sure. My manager agreed with what I was telling him but explained to me he didn't want conflict in the office, so I was to leave the two people alone for the time being."

"How did you respond to that?"

"Internally, I went berserk. I really couldn't believe what he was saying. I calmly asked him if he would be willing to speak to them, but he said no. Again, calmly, I suggested to him not doing anything would, in the long run, only create more conflict. But he didn't agree."

"What went through your mind at that point?" June asked.

"Honestly? I thought 'what a jerk!' I really like my manager. He's a great guy. He gave me the promotion in the first place. He really is the nicest guy you would ever want to meet. I felt bad I had such a strong reaction to him, but that is how I felt," Carolyn said.

"Then what did you do?"

"I went back and tried to talk to the two employees. I told them we all need to get along with one another, and I would do my best to support them. I also asked them to do their best to support me. That's when things went from bad to worse."

"What happened?"

"About two weeks later I decided to ask the two of them out to lunch as a good-will gesture. They not only said 'no,' but when I walked by the area they both work in, I heard them laughing. I could tell they were laughing at me. It's been that way for about two years now. That's why I want to leave. I've been trying to find another position for about six months, but there's nothing out there," she said.

"Would you like my thoughts?" June asked.

"Yes, of course," Carolyn replied.

"First, I am impressed with how quickly you have grown in your career. You're smart, hard working and I can tell you really care about people and the company you work for," June began.

"Thanks, June, I appreciate that."

"You've come a long way quickly, but if you are going to continue to grow you are going to have to learn better how to analyze your circumstances. Let me ask you a question and I want you to think about your answer before you respond. What do you think the adversity of your current situation is trying to teach you?" June asked.

"I'm not sure I understand your question."

"That reply tells me just how far away from the answer you really are. Try your best to answer my question," pressed June.

Carolyn sat quietly for several moments. I could see she was contemplating her answer. "Well, for one thing I think it's trying to teach me I shouldn't be working there anymore."

I took notice June rarely re-explained her questions to candidates who claimed to be confused. Instead, she presumed they did understand the question and then asked them to try harder to answer it. The amazing thing was they did answer her question without it having to be explained to them again! How she knew they had understood her in the first place was a complete mystery to me.

"You can do better than that," June said.

"Wow, you're tough June! I didn't expect this in an interview," Carolyn balked.

"Would you rather we just keep it superficial, so you don't have to really figure this thing out? I'm happy to do that if you wish. It will require a lot less of my time and energy," June said wryly.

"No, no, I do appreciate this. I just didn't know this is what we were going to be talking about." Carolyn spent a few more moments quietly thinking. Then she said, "I guess the other thing I learned is to listen to my instincts."

"What do you mean by that?"

"The day I had that conversation with my boss, I left our meeting feeling depressed. I knew doing nothing about the situation with the two employees was only going to make things worse, but I talked myself into trying his approach," she explained.

"Why do you think a smart young woman like you would try to talk herself into something she didn't believe in?"

"Well, I think I told myself maybe if I was, I don't know, nicer, I could fix the situation."

"So in other words, the problem wasn't so much with the two employees or your boss's need to avoid conflict. The problem was you weren't quite nice enough as a person. Is that right?" June asked.

"I knew I wasn't the only problem but, yes, it's true I started seeing myself as part of the problem," Carolyn confessed.

"Looking back on it, do you think that was an accurate assessment?" June asked.

"No, I don't. I just can't quite believe my boss would let such a good team go sour because he didn't want to deal with conflict. It makes me so angry he doesn't have more backbone!" she fumed.

"Do you know why that makes you so angry?"

"Yes, because it ruined a great situation."

"No, it makes you angry because you chose not to have backbone yourself. You knew the moment your boss chose to avoid the conflict, things were only going to get worse. But out of your own fear, your own lack of backbone, you talked yourself right out of your own beliefs. Rather than dealing with the situation correctly and honestly, which would have required courage on your part, you told yourself you were the problem. Once you made that decision, you became part of the problem. Of course they laughed at you when you tried to be nice to them. From their perspective, you were being weak and ridiculous," June said.

I was agreeing with June throughout the conversation until she said "you were being weak and ridiculous." That was just uncalled for. She didn't need to hit Carolyn below the belt when she had already made her point. I looked at Carolyn and, sure enough, she was crying. I knew this was going to happen.

"Yeah, you're right, June," Carolyn said. "I must have looked weak and ridiculous. I can't tell you how badly it made me feel every time I walked down the hall and heard their laughter or their nasty little comments. I really hate coming into work every day. I can't stand it!"

June handed Carolyn some tissue to wipe her tears, which didn't seem to be letting up any time soon. I felt badly for her. I wanted to say something to ease her pain, but I wasn't able to find the right words.

"Why do you think you chose to stay as long as you have?" June asked.

"I don't know. That's a really good question," Carolyn replied, still wiping away her tears.

"I know you have already made the decision to leave, so that's a good start. But to grow from this, you not only need to leave, you need to learn from the adversity you have been enduring. If you can understand what the adversity in your job is trying to tell you, you can turn this whole bad experience into a victory in no time," June explained.

Carolyn tears eased, and she was beginning to collect her composure. "That sounds good. How do I do that?"

"I want you to stop for a moment and really think about what might be the bigger lesson going on in all this?"

Carolyn stopped again to think about June's question. "Well, it helped when you pointed out I was acting just like my boss. You're right, I didn't have any backbone. Here I am always complaining to my friends about him, but I was doing the same thing. And on the other hand, I always tell everyone what a really nice guy he is. The truth is, the way he has managed me and other people in the company is not nice at all. So I guess I've learned that I have to have more backbone myself," she said.

"Okay, that's one lesson. Let me ask you another question, how has your work life been since you stopped being honest with yourself about your boss?" June asked.

"What do you mean?"

"After that first important conversation with your manager, you said you didn't listen to your instincts. How has your job gone since you decided not to listen to your instincts?"

"Not so well. That's probably the bigger lesson in all this. I haven't been honest with myself. No one prevented me from listening to my instincts. No one made me compromise myself. I did that, and I've been unhappy ever since. I've also been blaming others for my problems since that same time."

I noticed Carolyn was now sitting up straight and her confidence was building. I had been wrong again about June going too far in her sharp, forthright critique. Once again, she had somehow gotten away with it.

"Whenever we are not honest with ourselves, the world around us begins to break down. When I wasn't being honest with myself about my weight, that's when I gained so much. When I wasn't honest with myself about the kind of man I was marrying, that's when I ended up divorced. I had to learn that lesson three times," June explained.

"Wow, I didn't know you had been through all that. You seem so confident and happy," Carolyn said.

"I am, but I've worked very hard on myself. It's taken me years to learn how to be honest with myself. It's a lot of hard work. Brian here is just beginning the process," June said, looking over at me.

At first I was caught off guard. Why was she bringing me into it? I asked myself. I started telling Carolyn a little about my story and how I had really begun to grow since coming to work with June. I felt good about opening up and sharing. There was an amazing feeling in the air as the three of us talked about ourselves. It was one of the most real conversations I had ever been involved in with a candidate but, at the same time, it was easy. I felt free and happy. As I spoke, I also felt a strange closeness to both June and Carolyn. Each of us had some big flaws. Each of us had made some major bad decisions. But thanks to June's guidance and honesty, I had a sense we were all in it together. It was strange all this was taking place in an interview. The light started to go on. Maybe that's how she was able to pull off the "between the eyes" comments. She shared her flaws, too.

"When bad things are happening to us at work there is almost always a bigger lesson taking place – something important for us to learn. As bright and hard working as you are, you will never be fulfilled in your work life if you don't learn how to be honest with yourself. You also will never be happy unless you learn to have the courage to act on what you know is true," June explained.

"I would have never looked at it that way, June. Hearing it expressed that way, I can see I was resisting the bigger lesson and making myself miserable. I was so busy blaming my problems on everyone else, I never took the time to see what I was doing to contribute to my own misery," she said.

"It's never fun to be unhappy. When you understand the circumstances causing your dissatisfaction are perfectly designed for you to learn exactly what you need to learn in order to grow, everything changes. That's what those rare individuals who are fulfilled in life do so differently than the rest of the human race," June explained.

"Could you say that again? I really want to understand that point."

"Let me ask you. What would have happened if you would have been content not listening to your instincts? What would have happened to you if it hadn't bothered you that you lacked courage to act on your beliefs?" June asked.

"I probably would have just kept on going."

"Do you think you would have been happy?"

"I think I would have been okay."

"Is that what you really want in your career – to be 'okay'? Is that the dream you have for yourself?"

"No! Not by a long shot. I see what you're saying. If things hadn't gotten so bad, I never would have learned what I needed to learn to get what I really wanted out of my career. That makes a lot of sense. I never looked at it that way. That's funny. It's actually a very good thing everything went so badly," Carolyn said.

"Yes, it is. All things, especially the adversity we experience in our careers, are working to teach us the exact lessons we need to learn to realize our goals. I'm not saying every bad thing that happens to us is for the good. Sometimes bad things happen and they are just bad – things we can't make sense of. But most of the bad things that happen to us, if properly understood, are pointing us toward a better understanding of ourselves, our passions, our deepest desires and our dreams. That's how our careers work."

"You really believe that, June?"

"I don't believe it. I know it," June said smiling.

"You're saying even though we are all going through such frustration and confusion in our careers, most of it is happening for a reason?"

"Not just a reason. A reason that is perfectly designed to teach you the most important and essential lesson you require to move closer toward your goals and dreams," June clarified.

"It sounds like you're saying that God is the ultimate career counselor," Carolyn said laughing.

"What do you think?" June asked.

"Well, I'll have to think about that one! But something tells me you're probably right. This whole discussion has really opened my eyes. I need to rethink how I look at my career. Heck, I need to rethink how I look at my life!"

"That's why working for leadership you respect and, hopefully, are once in a while inspired by is the first priority in your job search. We need each other to interrupt the adversity that's happening to us. None of us can do it on our own. It takes wisdom and understanding to figure out the larger lessons that are taking place in our careers. Only great leadership can offer that," June explained.

"That's true. I don't have anyone in my life that can help me do that. How do you find people like that?"

"You have to understand how important they are to your success in life and then turn your focus and energies to trying to find them," June said.

"Are they really out there?"

"Yes, they are," June replied.

"I wish I was having an easier time believing that right now. I know there have been a lot of things I could have done better in my career, but it has always seemed to me that, at the end of the day, I was on my own."

"That's up to you. If you continue to hold on to that belief, then you will continue to make decisions that prove it to be true. On the other hand, if you dig deeper and apply what you've learned here today, you can begin to change that belief and look for leadership that has backbone and integrity. You can find leadership, through their sense of commitment and involvement, convinces you that you are not on your own. If you make it your number one priority and seek it with everything you have, you'll find it," June said.

"When you put it that way, yes, I can see how my beliefs about people and life are at the heart of my difficulties at work. I'll tell you though, as you were just talking, I could see myself setting my mind to go after great leadership. I can see myself working for the kind of people you just described. I can also see that if I got off track and talked myself into wanting money or title or promises of growth or anything else as my top priority, then I would put myself right back into the same adversity I'm in right now. I can also see how adversity would be exactly what I needed to get back on track."

"You've got it," June said.

"Why do you think I had to stay in the job even after I decided I wanted to leave over six months ago? Why do you think nothing has come up for me?" Carolyn asked.

"How long did you lie to yourself before deciding to leave?" June asked.

"Oh, I guess about a year."

"Now, if you really cared about someone very deeply, and you wanted to teach them a very critical lesson, would you give them what they wanted the moment they figured out they had been off track?" June asked.

"Well, I would be tempted to but, no, if I really wanted to make sure they wouldn't repeat their mistake, I wouldn't give them what they wanted right away," Carolyn replied.

"You see, that's the situation you are in. The larger lesson is crucial to your future success and fulfillment. It's important you appreciate the magnitude. You spent a year ignoring your instincts, living in fear, being dishonest with yourself and, overall, treating yourself very poorly. Now you've spent the last six months trying to get out. What do you imagine is the larger lesson of these last six months?"

"I would say it's pointing out just how important all the things you're talking about really are. There is a price to pay for not doing what I know is right. I think I'm paying that price, but I can use this to get even more motivated than I was coming in here today. Also, I didn't understand the larger lesson so, until I understood what was really happening to me and why it was happening, it wouldn't have done me a whole lot of good to find a new position," Carolyn concluded.

"That's right. One of my favorite sayings is, 'Show me someone who wants to learn and I'll show you an amateur!' Now you have arrived at a deeper understanding and it's high time you move on to a position that will bring you fulfillment," June said.

The rest of the interview was spent talking about the position with my new client. Carolyn sounded very excited about the opportunity. When June started going in on a candidate, it felt as though all time and space were changing. The three of us were no longer in an interview. We weren't in the professional world talking about jobs and careers. We were in some other reality where we were talking about the deepest of truths, not just about jobs and careers, but about our true selves, our pains and limitations as well as our desires and dreams. Then when it was all over, we would re-enter the professional world. That's where we were now, back in the real world discussing the new job.

But this time, rather than being anxious about how the interview was going, I was actually regretting the fact we had to return from the place June had taken us. It was a place I had always dreamed of but didn't know really existed. A place where we all got to be our true selves – a place where even though we had to hear and admit to some of our *horrible faults*, we got to enjoy one another and experience a great intimacy. An intimacy we all knew we had always been designed for but had somehow lost. It was in this world, June's world, where remarkable change happened. Real change – the kind that could last a lifetime.

"The first rule of good interviewing: There is nothing to think about, worry about or analyze until you have an offer."
June Gregory

Brian

Loneliness is a Strange Consequence of Growth

Something happens when you make an important choice. Once I returned to work for June I could feel a subtle, but significant, change in myself. I felt calmer, more relaxed and less intense. I had bet on the single bright dot and I was committed to it. Intellectually, I still had no idea if I had made the right choice, but I had finally made my decision and, so far, it felt good. I had also withstood June's two-hour onslaught about my lack of character surprisingly well! Typically, when June started giving me her special version of constructive criticism, I would immediately feel overwhelmed and defensive. But this time I took it all, not that I understood much of what she was trying to teach me about my faults. Nor did I entirely comprehend what she was trying to tell me about what it would cost me in life if I didn't grow up and out of these weaknesses. But I knew June well enough to know if she was upset it meant that she had not completely given up on me.

As good as I felt about having my job back, I knew I still had another big hurdle to clear before my already long day would end. I still had to go home and face Robin and my friends' disappointment. I also had to call my dad and tell him I had not listened to his advice and hear his predictable condescending reaction. I had to see the looks of utter disgust on the faces of my wife and friends as I told them I had not quit as I said I would. Going home meant talking to and being around people who truly believed I was an idiot for continuing to work for June.

It was on my second drive home that day I realized that my work life with June and my personal life with my friends and family were in complete and utter conflict. Not one person in my personal life understood my excitement about working for her. No one seemed to care about the positive changes in me. Not a single one of my friends or family seemed to understand what it meant to me to be working for an individual who was as strong, honest and as giving as June. They listened to my stories of how June was having a profound impact on my life, but they could not figure out why she was so concerned about my character and why she wasn't paying me a salary. Perhaps it was the manner in which I explained my excitement about my job, but no one trusted what June was doing for me.

On the other hand, when I told June about my friends' and family's reaction to my job, she couldn't, for the life of her, understand their reaction. What kind of people would want to see me stay defeated and unhappy? What kind of people would not support me in learning how to be honest with myself? Why would they not want me to learn how to take responsibility for my choices, to learn how to make my way in the business world, and to earn a good living? Who were these people who had the gall to object to me finally learning how to gain some self-respect? She was horrified anyone's spouse, family or friends could appear so self-centered and negative. "It sure explains why you turned out the way you have," she once told me with a sense of real compassion.

June also could not understand why I would want to continue to be close to these people. Why would I want to be around people who wanted to see me fail even if they were related to me? "Who needs family and friends like that? I'd rather be alone," she'd tell me. So there it was: my wife, friends and relatives felt June was some weirdo I was allowing to take advantage of me. In turn, June saw a group of people so negative they would rather see me unhappy for the rest of my life than encourage me to take some risks to challenge my negatives.

I was coming to the realization there was no way to reconcile the dissonance in my work and personal lives. There was simply no way for me to exist in both worlds. When I let my family and friends influence me, I would begin to question my choice to work for June. I knew I couldn't continue to let that happen. I had made a promise to myself, and I was determined to keep it. The more I talked to June about my family and friends, the more I was seeing what unhappy people they really were. They were all like me. They were people who believed in playing it safe in life and wallowing in their past hurts and failures. Like me, they felt poorly about themselves where it really mattered and pretended to have it together in the areas that didn't have much meaning. They were focused on money or status or both. Like me, they were not honest about their fears and weaknesses. Not one of them had taken a risk in order to grow. For my family and friends, "work" meant being unhappy in order to make money and increase your status. For June, a career meant being committed and working hard to grow as a person and helping others do the same. It was no wonder that each side didn't like or trust the other – our core values about life and work were the exact opposite.

The more I thought about this conflict, the more I began to realize that June was right. Like the person I was before I met June, my circle of influence was essentially negative. I still found a sense of comfort and belonging in being around them, but it was at the cost of my well-being and growth. With June my inner world mattered, and it was slowly improving. With my friends and family, my outer world mattered while my inner didn't seem to have much importance. The clearer I became, the less I wanted to spend time with them. Although it was just beginning to form, I had a very real sense that anyone who did not understand my motivations for working for June was to be avoided. This didn't do a whole lot to help my already-strained marriage.

A few days went by and, thankfully, June started warming up to me again. I was continuing to make my cold calls. Although I wasn't making placements, I was continuing to improve. I wasn't thinking about my money problems for a change. I was just focused on doing the best job I could and enjoying the fact I was still working for June. Eventually we resumed our end-of-the-day talks. I felt I was getting back on track.

As my relationship with June improved, my need for separating from negative people also increased. I began to avoid friends and family. On the one hand, I found this separation to be freeing. On the other, it was very difficult. I could add loneliness to the list of challenges my new job was presenting to me. I desperately wanted to talk to someone, anyone, about the positive changes I was experiencing. But there was no one to talk to – no one other than June to encourage me.

On a drive home I remember asking myself, "What kind of God punishes a good decision with poverty, ridicule, rejection, rough commutes and now, the loss of friends and family?" The more I thought about the question, the more I started feeling sorry for myself. The next day I very carefully brought up the question to June. Her answer was simple and clear. "What have you really lost?" she inquired.

I had never had money or known how to make it. As long as I could remember, I had felt tremendously insecure and rejected. The truth was I didn't even really like the friends and family from whom I was separating. It never ceased to amaze me how I could talk myself into feeling like a victim whenever I had to take on a new challenge. June was, of course, absolutely right. I had not been punished by God for making a good decision. I had already been broke, ridiculed, and rejected before I went to work for June. What was new in my life was a very real and completely unfamiliar sense that I could grow. What was new was the vague possibility I could escape the fears and torment that haunted me. What was new was the possibility of putting *me* back together again. No, I didn't like the lack of money, ridicule, rejection, excessive commute or the loneliness. But God was not punishing me. Far from it, He was reaching out to lift me up and give me a chance.

It was at this time June taught me another very important aspect about growth. "Don't eliminate everyone from your life, even if they are negative," she told me during one of our conversations. "You need to change slowly, one step at a time. If you take on too many changes, you won't make it. Hang on to some of your friends and family, and slowly over time begin to replace them with more positive people. You need to let go of the people who really bring you down like your father, for instance, but you shouldn't let go of everyone."

She also explained to me what she meant by letting go of a relationship. "You need to learn how to tell the people in your life that are really negative that you are going to take a vacation from the relationship for a while. Don't be dramatic and tell them that you don't want to see them ever again. Just take a vacation. Tell your dad that you're going to take a six-month break. In six months, you can revisit the relationship. Although, I've got to tell you, your dad has some serious problems. After hearing what he has done in the past, I can't imagine him coming around. But you never know for certain about people. The point is you need to learn to treat yourself well. By taking vacations from the negative people in your life, you allow yourself to grow and avoid the drama."

June also taught me how to set time boundaries with people. "If you're going to see someone whom you know can be negative, make sure to have an escape plan. Ask a friend to call you every fifteen minutes. If the negative person is still being enjoyable, tell your friend that you are with someone and to call you back in another fifteen minutes. As soon as your interaction begins to go wrong, politely let them know you need to go and see the person who has been calling you. Don't pretend. Really go see that person. That way you can keep control."

It was amazing to me just how well June's ideas worked. My dad didn't seem to mind when I told him I thought it would be the best thing for our relationship if we took a vacation for awhile. Setting up time boundaries with other friends and family members had a remarkable effect on my relationships. Suddenly the negative people weren't so negative. It was as though they somehow knew that if they started judging me or putting me down, I wasn't going to stick around as I had done in the past. I felt they were giving me their best efforts. Some could last thirty minutes or more before they would "go south" on me. And instead of getting upset with them, I told them I had to go, as June had suggested. It was so simple! I was suddenly able to bring order to my usually helter-skelter, roller-coaster life.

I was also beginning to understand what June meant by learning to treat myself better. As I learned to take more "vacations" from people when they were really bad and to set time boundaries and have escape plans from my questionable relationships, I sensed that people were beginning to respect and like me more. Not only was I happier, but I was getting the respect I had always yearned for. This was the feeling of self-respect June had been trying to teach me.

Even with the new tools June had given me, I found myself feeling very much alone in my life outside of work. I no longer belonged to my old world. Other than June, I didn't know anyone who really understood the new challenges I was facing or the positive changes I was experiencing. Even though I understood that everything happening to me was improving my world, it was a tremendously difficult realization that one of the costs of my growth would be the feeling I no longer belonged to a family or group of friends.

Loneliness is a strange consequence of growth. But this was the result of my choice, and I was determined not to turn back. One by one, the dark dots were slowly leaving my world. As each dot left I was a little more alone, but I was also beginning to understand an amazing new reality. The light was becoming brighter. What had started out as a momentary, fleeting flash was growing into a small area of light I could count on. My outside world was being slowly torn apart while my inner world was beginning to come to life.

It had only been a matter of weeks since my revelation in the car and decision to continue to work for June, but I was fully aware of just how much I had already been rewarded for making the right choice. I had all kinds of financial problems, but I had never felt better. Thinking back on how I had told my dad that I had decided to keep my job, I was already able to laugh about it.

"Hi, Dad, I'm calling to let you know that I've decided to continue to work for June. I took your advice and gave her the ultimatum you suggested. But when I did it, I felt lousy right down to my very core. I know you think I'm being weak and allowing her to take advantage of me. I don't think so, Dad. I went back and begged for my job. The more I begged, the better I started feeling. Thankfully, she agreed to give me one more chance. You see, Dad, the longer I work for her, the better I feel about myself. That's the part I can't seem to get you or anyone else to understand. Anyway that's it. I just wanted to let you know what was going on. Oh, by the way, I think it might be a good idea if we each take a vacation from our relationship for a few months. I believe we could both benefit from some time off. Take care."

I was so glad that I got his answering machine!

Vicky

Vicky had been referred to June by her father whom June had placed several years earlier. June especially seemed to love dealing with second-generation candidates and had always given them extra attention. Vicky came in during the late afternoon, and June asked me if I would like to sit in on the interview.

Wearing a nice suit, Vicky made a very positive first impression. June greeted her in her usual manner and the two of them starting talking about Vicky's father. June spent several minutes telling her how impressed she had been with her dad. They shared some stories and then got down to the business of interviewing.

Vicky had been in the banking field for eight and a half years. She had started her first job when she was 18 years old and stayed with that bank for seven years. She had been with her present bank for just under two years. The bank had just gone through a complete change of management. The new management team had decided to eliminate Vicky's position.

"How did you feel when you lost your job?" June asked.

"Well, to be honest, it was okay. I didn't like the new management very much anyway. They seemed very rigid in the way they did things," she answered.

"Why did you leave your first position?" June asked.

"I felt that no matter how much I had grown, they were always going to see me as the 18-year-old girl who had started with them seven years earlier," she explained.

"That's unfortunate, but happens a lot. In those circumstances you really are forced into leaving in order to grow," June said. "Tell me about your ideal position?"

"I'm really very open to anything that sounds interesting," she answered.

June then went over Vicky's strengths and weaknesses. I was impressed with Vicky's ability to articulate her strong points. It was becoming clear she had a lot to offer in terms of her skills and professionalism.

"Okay, I see that you are making $50,000 now. What's your minimum salary, if you saw your ideal opportunity?" June inquired.

"I'd really like at least $60,000. If it was a really great opportunity though, I might consider $58,000," she answered.

"Did you believe you were underpaid?' June asked.

"I'm not sure. I think I was paid fairly."

"Then let me ask you. Why do you think you are worth more money? Usually, being let go by your employer doesn't make you worth more."

With June's question, the room chilled noticeably. June had fired her first shot, and suddenly things weren't so friendly. Vicky sat quietly, her eyes looking downward. It was clear her feelings had been hurt. She was struggling to respond.

June, however, wasn't about to back off. "Okay, if you can't answer that question, let me ask you another. Were you happy in your last position?"

"Until the new management came in, I was comfortable," Vicky replied still looking down.

"Listen, if I'm going to help you, you are going to have to look up at me," June said.

Vicky lifted her eyes to look at June.

"On a scale of 1 to 10 with 10 being the most fulfilled you can imagine being in a job, what number would you give your last position before the management change took place?" June asked.

Again Vicky sat quietly. This time I could tell she was really thinking about June's question.

"I guess I would give them a 6," she said quietly.

"And your position before that, what would you give them?' June asked.

"Oh, I would give them a 9. They were great people to work for," she said.

"You told me they failed to recognize your growth over the seven years you worked for them. Is that right?" June pressed.

"Yes," she replied.

"A moment ago I asked you if you were happy and you responded by telling me you were comfortable. Do you believe being comfortable and being happy are the same thing?" June asked.

"I don't know. I hadn't thought about it," she replied.

With each new question, Vicky was becoming more passive. June, on the other hand, was just revving up. I had been on the receiving end of this type of conversation with June. I felt like I was watching someone hold out a big piece of raw meat to a hungry lion. Vicky's passivity was the meat and June's desire to help her to stop compromising had all the passion of a hungry lion.

"Vicky, would you like my thoughts?" June asked.

"Yes, I would."

This response always surprised me. June had already zapped Vicky for asking for a higher salary than when she had been let go. Right or wrong, Vicky was hurt by June's comment. Yet, Vicky, like every other candidate, wanted to hear what June had to say. Did the candidates not understand what was coming? A warning shot had already gone off. How could they not comprehend that June was about to shred their fragile ego into tiny bits? Or did the candidates understand the onslaught their egos were about to receive but wanted to hear it anyway? I quickly came to the conclusion the candidates must be falling for the same "trap" I was always falling into. They were so conditioned to hearing "nice" feedback; they assumed June was going to tell them something they could handle. In June's case, that was a very bad assumption.

"I'd like to know what you are so afraid of."

"I'm not sure," Vicky replied, looking confused by the question.

"Okay, if you can't answer that question, then let me ask you another. Do you think being comfortable means being safe?" she asked.

"Yes, I would say so," she replied.

"And you were comfortable in your last job?" June pressed.

"Yes, I didn't like the new management, but I still felt comfortable."

"If comfortable is safe, then how do you explain being fired?"

"I don't know."

"Let me tell you something, and I really want you to listen carefully. Are you listening?" June asked.

"Yes," she replied attentively.

"In your work life, the most dangerous place you can be is 'comfortable.' If you're comfortable, you're not safe. The fact you were fired is just one way the danger showed itself. It could have showed up in your lack of motivation, energy, passion, marketability, or frustration to name just a few.

"I hadn't looked at it that way," Vicky responded.

"In your past two positions, when did you realize that you were no longer challenged and the situation was not going to change? I want you to take a moment to think about your answer."

I could see that Vicky was taking the question seriously.

"I would say in my first position I knew after about two years. In this position, I could tell after three or four months," she answered.

It always surprised me how candidates who appeared to be so passive and unaware of themselves could respond to this type of question with such clarity and certainty.

"And what did you decide to do once you knew?"

"Well, I guess, I decided not to do anything," she said shyly.

"Why do you think that is?"

There was a long uncomfortable silence as Vicky sat in her chair thinking about the question. The good news was I could see she was really trying to figure it out. Then, by the look on her face, I could see she had hit upon something.

"Because I never thought of it in terms of being happy," she said. Suddenly, Vicky straightened up in her chair and began to speak up. "I just figured I was comfortable and that was enough."

"Is it enough?"

Vicky was thinking again.

"No, June, it's not enough," she said with determination. "I would love to have a job where I was challenged and appreciated. I don't need to feel that way every moment of every day, but I sure would like a lot more of it than I've had for the last six years."

"Are you willing to do what it takes to go after that kind of job?" June asked.

"Yes, I think so. I grew up in a large family where all I ever saw was people playing it safe. Most of my family is in finance, and they all have jobs where they feel comfortable. I don't think any of them are really happy. I would love to go after a position where I could be happy. I just never thought that I could have that. And the truth is, even if I had known what I wanted, I've lacked the confidence to go for it."

"Do you know how to get confidence?" June asked.

"No, but that's a really good question. I've never heard anyone talk about how to get it."

I had to admit I had never thought about that question either. I would kill to have more confidence. Outwardly, for appearance's sake, I was sitting there as if I already knew the answer. Inwardly I was shouting, "Please, give me the answer. I'm desperate!"

"You gain confidence when you choose to have the courage to do something you didn't think you could do. You grow in confidence when you exercise your courage. There is no other way to acquire it. Before you learned to drive a car you probably didn't have any confidence you could drive. Once you got behind the wheel and drove, you developed the confidence you could drive. If your fear was so great you never attempted to drive, you would never develop the confidence you now have as a driver. Most of us are so confident about our ability to drive we don't even remember just how much fear we had the first time we took the wheel," June explained.

"That makes sense. I think when it comes to having more confidence at work I've just been hoping it would show up. But it never does."

"That is how most people handle the issue of confidence in their careers. They believe confidence comes from learning. They hold on to some false belief they would become more confident if they were only more educated, more experienced, smarter or more assertive. The list goes on and on. The truth is confidence only comes from having the courage to do something we didn't think we could do. The only true assumption about confidence is we can have more of it anytime we choose to be more courageous. That means you can become more confident any time you like, even this very moment," June said.

"I've never thought about it like that before. I guess I come from a family that is afraid to take chances – to be courageous. They don't challenge themselves."

"What about you? What are you afraid of doing?" June asked.

Vicky looked perplexed, but seemed determined to answer the question.

"I think I've been afraid to take chances in my jobs. I don't ask for what I really want because I'm afraid that they are going to say 'no.' Because I don't speak up, I end up doing the job no one else wants to do. I guess when it comes down to it, I'm afraid of rejection. I don't take chances where I might be rejected."

"That must have taken some courage to admit," June said.

"Yes, it did!" Vicky said smiling. "I've never admitted that to anyone before."

"Would you like to try a little exercise that may help you with your fear?"

"Yes, I would."

"I want you to take a moment and imagine what the next ten years of your career will look like if you do not change your fear of rejection. Shut your eyes and see yourself ten years from now. How do you look, how you feel, what it's like to wake up on a Monday morning? Let me know when you think you've got the image."

After about a minute or two, Vicky told June she had the image.

"Good. Now I want you close your eyes again. This time, I want you to imagine yourself ten years from now, but this time I want you to see yourself having spent these next ten years living without the fear of rejection. Notice how you look and feel and what it's like to wake up on a Monday morning. Let me know when you have it."

I watched Vicky as she sat there in her chair, obediently following June's strange exercise. As the moments went by, I saw a smile come over her face. She no longer looked like the passive woman who had been struggling just minutes before. She looked stronger and surer of herself.

"How did that feel?" June asked.

"It felt great, June. In fact, I don't know that I've ever felt that good before!"

"Do you understand what it's going to take for you to be that Vicky instead of the first one you saw?"

"Yes, I'm going to have to be brave enough to speak up for myself."

"And what else?" June asked.

Vicky thought for a moment. "I'm going to have to stop playing it safe. If a job isn't right for me, I need to take action rather than just allowing myself to be comfortable."

"Good for you! The most unsafe position in your work life is a situation where you are not growing. Growth is never comfortable. It always demands that you give more of yourself than you are comfortable giving. We all need to be in environments that are challenging us. No position is perfect, but we have to be honest with ourselves about what is healthy and what isn't," June explained.

"It was so easy for me to settle on being comfortable. But all it ended up doing for me was getting me fired. I don't want to settle for that again," Vicky said.

"They did you a favor by letting you go. How else would you have learned?"

"That's true. That's how I'm going to look at it."

"I have a plaque that I love. Where is it?" June looked around her desk. "Here it is." June held up the plaque so both Vicky and I could see it. It read, *"If you are being kicked out of town, get to the head of the line and call it a parade."* June laughed as Vicky read it out loud.

"I just love that saying!" June choked, in the middle of one of her full-body-shaking laughs.

"That's great! I'm going to keep that one in mind," Vicky said.

"The greatest obstacle to finding a great job is not being in a bad one. It's being in a comfortable one. We settle for 'good enough' when we deeply desire the exceptional. When it's obvious that we are in a bad situation, most of us know we want to make a change. The problem comes when, as in your situation, we are comfortable in a position meeting our basic needs, and we believe that's all we deserve to have," June explained.

"That's exactly what happened to me," Vicky replied.

"Now I am going to give you another chance to answer my questions. We can pretend we are starting over. Would you like that?" June asked.

"Yes, very much, June."

"What is your ideal position?" June asked.

"I would love a position where I can utilize my skills and experience in a great environment. It would be the kind of company where, as I bettered myself, there would be the opportunity to contribute more. Does that sound better?"

"Does that sound better to you?" June asked.

"Yes, it does." Vicky looked as though she was proud of her new response.

"Well then, there's your answer. I thought it was a great answer. Brian, what do you think?"

"I thought it was great, too," I chimed in.

"If you saw your ideal position, what salary would you consider?" June asked.

"If it were a great opportunity, I think I could live on something in the high forty's. I'd have to really budget, but I'd manage," she answered.

"Taking less money to get the job you really wanted would take some courage," June replied.

Just twenty minutes ago, Vicky had looked so unhappy when she told June that her minimum salary was $58,000. Now she looked almost radiant as she committed to a minimum salary $10,000 less.

"Thanks, June. It feels good to start believing in myself for a change," she said.

"Now that you have a better understanding of what you want in your career, what numbers would you give your last two companies?" June asked.

"Good question. I would give my last job a 4 or a 5 and my first company a 6. I know I was afraid to speak up, but both of them did very little to help me grow," she said.

"Those numbers are more accurate to the situation you described. Now I want you to go home and work on seeing your fearless self who is employed by a great company. I'll call you when the opportunity comes up. Do we have a deal?" June asked.

"That sounds great, June. Thank you for all your help. I probably would have spent most of my career running scared of rejection if you hadn't taken the time to help me. I really appreciate it. My dad said you were great, but I had no idea anyone could help me this much. This hasn't been a normal interview. That's for sure," she said.

On my ride home that night I found myself thinking about what Vicky had said about spending her entire career living in fear of rejection. She was right. Besides June, who else had the wisdom, time and desire to help her overcome her fear? And what if Vicky had spent her career captive to her fear? What a sad waste that would have been. June wasn't just having encouraging talks with candidates. She was setting them on an entirely new course for their lives. She was successfully connecting them back to their desires and potential by teaching them to use their courage to overcome their fears.

Then there was the issue of the candidate's marketability. Vicky, with her lack of confidence and a $60,000 asking price, was not a marketable candidate. She either would have found an extremely poorly managed company or, most likely, no job at all. After speaking with June, she was not only more confident, her salary was more flexible as well. It was mind blowing to think, in just a few minutes, how much more marketable she had become.

I knew helping people overcome their fears was the key to making them more marketable. I was having a difficult time however, imagining that someday I would capable of helping someone in the manner June had just helped Vicky.

I took a moment to try and imagine myself ten years in the future, having overcome my fears. I had to do this while driving, so I couldn't close my eyes. Nothing happened at first, but then slowly a feeling of strength crept over me. It was a great feeling. Then a question came to my mind: *If I can make myself feel this way right now, why can't I make myself feel this way whenever I choose?*

I must have been lost in thought. I didn't notice the car to my immediate left was moving in to my lane. I honked my horn just in time to get his attention and avert an accident. I was mad! The stupid driver hadn't even been paying attention and could have caused a real pile-up. Maybe that's why I can't hang on to the feeling of living without my fears. *There are just too many stupid people to be afraid of*, I thought.

Brian

With my new abilities to set boundaries in place, my confidence at work was increasing. I was no longer afraid of the job. I was still intimidated at the prospect of making cold calls, and I knew June would most likely discover another one of my shortcomings at any moment. But I was beginning to feel comfortable coming to work each day.

There was one rather overwhelming problem. I couldn't make a placement! Even with all of June's help, I could not, for the life of me, recruit a candidate and place them. The venture capital firm would have hired Jennifer, but at the last minute their current receptionist decided to stay. It wasn't a matter of failing to understand the positions I was recruiting for. Thanks to June's long talks, I was getting a better idea of what I was presenting on the phone. She was great at explaining to me the responsibilities of the positions. So despite my total lack of business knowledge, I was getting pretty good at faking it on the phone – a skill I picked up in my previous life as a phony. The people I was calling no longer sounded as though they felt sorry for me. As June was helping me gain a better understanding of the business and the positions for which I was recruiting, people started to treat the phone conversations more seriously. They were taking the time to think about who they might know that would be a good match for the opportunity I was presenting.

I couldn't blame my inability to make a placement on my fear of rejection either. The seven months I had spent working for June had already changed me into a much more relaxed and far less insecure person. It was clear to me having listened to June, and making the choices I made, I had grown quite a bit in a relatively short period of time. The growth was even more magnified for me because I had come from a world where everyone, especially me, talked about growth but never made the difficult choices or took the risks required to see any tangible change. The growth I was experiencing was real. It changed what I felt, not just my thoughts.

It was interesting to me that before I met June, growth had been a purely intellectual pursuit. I spent a lot of time talking about politics, philosophy and other peoples' problems. It was a mind set of "if the world would only change in this way or that, then we would all be happier." (Especially me!) In my life before June, my happiness and well-being was completely dependent on circumstances beyond my control. I was dependent on what other people thought of me ("Hi, Mom and Dad"). At the core, it was a life of trying to gain love and respect by impressing others. In life with June, the world changed only if I changed. June was concerned with my inner world where my ability to be honest with myself, my courage, integrity and self-respect were the focus. My life could only improve if I improved. The world of my fears, doubts, insecurities and choices was exposed and up for discussion and review. The world of my behaviors, emotions and, here's the big one; the world of my HONEST THOUGHTS is where June lived. Compared to my "Before June" life, I was growing by leaps and bounds.

No, my inability to make a placement – or money – was not an issue of having not grown professionally or personally. From my point of view, it was purely a case of really bad luck. It seemed the closer I got to placing a candidate, the more bizarre the reasons would be for the placement to go wrong. Besides Jennifer, there was the candidate who desperately wanted my client's job offer. After an extensive two weeks of interviewing, the day finally arrived when she got the offer (placement!). Later that same day she found out her husband was being transferred to another state, so she had to turn down the offer (no placement).

There was the very bright, straight-laced Harvard graduate who received an offer (placement!). She accepted and it looked like I finally had some money to pay my bills, only to find out the next day she had not passed her background check. She had apparently put herself though Harvard by working as a call girl! To her "complete surprise," her police record showed up on the background check (no placement, no money, growing bills).

There was the candidate who worked for a boss who was constantly lying to her. She hated her job and her boss. She begged me to help her find a better company to work for. I was able to help her find a great new position working for wonderful people (placement!). She was thrilled to be going to work for people who would respect her and treat her with dignity. But when she went to give notice to her "he's just awful, I can't stand being around him" boss, he told her he really needed her and promised to try to change. Somehow she believed him and told me, and the great company I had found for her, she had changed her mind and was going to stay at her current employer (no placement!).

This series of incredibly bad luck felt remarkably unfair. Here I am making healthy decisions, trying to do the right thing, and all I get is: a woman who pursues a job while having no idea what is going on in her husband's career, an intelligent, straight-laced Harvard graduate who is majoring in prostitution, and a very insecure woman who actually believes the boss she so desperately wants to get away from …because he lies! What made matters even worse was as each placement looked like it was going to come together, I would promise the people I owed money to that I was going to pay them. With each quirky failure, I had to go back and explain to my debtors that I couldn't pay them as I had promised. Needless to say, this "I can pay you…" and then "uh, you won't believe what happened, sorry, I can't pay you" approach to my finances did NOT go over well at all. I needed to make money and the pressure was, again, becoming overwhelming.

As placements continued to find strange ways to go wrong, and with the continual pressure to make money, the doubts about the job and my ability to grow began to resurface. Maybe I wasn't supposed to be one of the lucky people in life. Financially, the only thing I had managed to do right was to get into a car accident. *There are happy people, like June, and unhappy people like me*, I remember thinking. How else can you explain these strange events? All you needed was one thing to go right and you would know that working for June was the right thing. But nothing has gone right. Given *everything* is going wrong, you have to admit you are not going to make it. Remember when they all implied I was going to end up being a broke idiot? Well, isn't that exactly what is happening? These were the thoughts that were beginning to enter and slowly take over my mind.

"A broke idiot." The words were harsh, but the reality felt so real. I spent hours, day after day, fearing the possibility of failure. I could see myself living on the streets, a 23-year-old in a strained marriage with an infant – a man without money, without family or friends, or a place to live. That was my fear. Each placement that went wrong was telling me this fear was slowly becoming a reality. My dad, family and friends had only been trying to warn me about this inevitable truth. What June was saying was right, but it didn't apply to someone like me. People like me just had to try to survive, to work to stay off the streets. My type worked to keep the wolves at bay, to keep our fears from becoming realities. People like June, on the other hand, were different. It was easy for them to make money. They could afford to take chances and talk about "growth" and "happiness." People like June were lucky; people like me weren't. Fundamentally, there was just something right and good about some people and something wrong and messed up about others. I had been born on the wrong side of the equation. It was that simple.

As the circumstances of losing placements continued to become more bizarre, I saw it as a confirmation of my worst fears. On my drive to and from work, I spent a lot of time thinking about why things were going wrong. Being a former philosophy student, I would always overanalyze any unresolved issue. And the more I thought about it, the more I came to the conclusion that it was God (although I didn't think about Him very often) who was responsible for these placements not happening. It was the same God who had messed things up for me in the first place. He was the one who gave me an emotionally-disturbed mom and a checked-out dad who betrayed me. He gave me the speech impediment as a kid. He didn't care that I felt so lousy much of the time. And it was God who was orchestrating these strange circumstances to ensure these placements would not happen. It was God who was making sure I wouldn't make any money.

Who else, I reasoned, could make everything that could go wrong, go wrong? Who else had the power? God wanted me to be a broke idiot. And if that's what He wanted, then that's the way it was going to be. Some people have it; some don't. Although I could never admit it, I hated Him for that, really hated Him.

It was during this time of inner torment my secret idea of God's campaign of persecution against me came spilling out in one of my talks with June. The conversation was a very strange one. By this time, I knew exactly how June would respond to anyone who went into a victim mode to describe their circumstances. By now, I had seen it time and again. She would let candidates tell their story, careful never to interrupt them. Then she would ask if they would like to hear her thoughts. Since most candidates were used to getting a sympathetic ear when they expressed their problems, they would enthusiastically ask for her feedback. Then, in a very nice, but forceful tone, POW, WHAM! June would give it to them right between the eyes! She would go into a powerful diatribe pointing out the choices they had made throughout their careers and how they had been free to make those choices. She would then show them how they were placing the blame for their problems and mistakes on everyone except themselves. She would go through each poor decision they had made in their careers and point out how they, according to their own accounts, had strong indications of problems with the company during the initial interview process. She could show candidates that, if they were going to be honest with themselves, they had been aware of the problems with their new employer before they accepted the position. She went on to talk to them about how they had decided to take the position despite these warning signs and how they were now blaming the company for a decision they had never felt good about in the first place. She looked them in the eyes and told them that they were acting like victims, and they would never grow to realize their incredible potential unless they learned to take responsibility for their choices and to listen to and act on their instincts.

So keeping June's predictable reaction in mind, and yet desperately needing her help, I knew I had to somehow communicate without setting her off. It seemed to me that I was forever making her work very hard to help me figure out what should have been obvious. My sensitivities and defenses were thoroughly entrenched. Reacting to her efforts to help me by behaving as though I was under attack, I made it nearly impossible for June to help me without giving her a hassle. And once I did figure out what she was trying to tell me, I always felt stupid and ridiculous for resisting her so fervently. This time I was very aware of not wanting to make her angry with me. The more I thought about it, the more I came to realize I was trying to figure out how I could talk to her about being a victim without sounding like one? *Is that even possible?* I wondered. That's the dance I was trying to figure out the moves to. I had a long drive home and another back to work the next morning to figure it out.

When I arrived at work the next day, I realized for all the time I had spent pondering the question, I hadn't really come up with a solution. In my mind I had gone over all the different ways the conversation could go poorly, but I hadn't figured out a way to talk to June that didn't sound whiney. I was not prepared, but I knew I had to talk to her. I was sure that she had already picked up on my conflict and doubt. She could sense those things even before I was aware of them. I knew if I didn't take the initiative to talk to her, she would call me out on my poor attitude and that would only add to her frustration with me. It was up to me to bring it up.

As was her custom, June got into the office a little late. Usually we would talk for a few minutes then go to work. But this particular morning was different. She was especially joyful having just purchased a new piece of jewelry she was ecstatic about. I knew about as much about expensive jewelry as I knew about brain surgery, so I had to act excited for her. She was absolutely delighted with her new ring. She was just like a little girl with her favorite new doll. Her eyes sparkled as she spoke. Like a child, she wanted me to understand everything about it: what kind of stone it was, where it came from, why the color was unique, how she found it, etc. I just sat and listened, careful to nod my head and smile at the right moments. She was joy. I was torment. What a contrast! After ten minutes or so, she looked up from her ring and asked me how I was doing. "You don't seem yourself this morning," she said.

How she could tell I wasn't doing well while being completely engrossed in her new jewelry caught me off guard. Nevertheless, I knew this was it. I had hoped I would have had until the end of the day, but here it was. It was time to talk to June.

"June, I really like my job and I feel I'm learning a lot." I had a brief flashback to the conversation where I gave her my ultimatum, but I immediately made myself stop thinking about that disaster. "I want you to know I am very grateful for everything you are teaching me." I was aware I didn't really mean that at that moment but I was still, for some reason, very glad I had said it. "I was just wondering if you had some insight as to why my placements are not coming together. Is there something wrong with me? Do you think I just might not be cut out for this job?" *Pray that this works, Brian.*

That was it. I was done. After almost 24 hours of thought about how I could ask June the question, "Why am I a victim?" without sounding like one, all I had come up with was, "What's wrong with me?" The words had just come out of their own accord. I sat there waiting for the onslaught. I had gotten up the nerve, once again, to bother her with my negativity. I knew what was coming and, for the first time, I somehow felt prepared for it.

But then something very strange happened. June wasn't mad or disappointed in me. She didn't call me out on my fears, dishonesty or negative thinking. June looked me in the eyes and said, "Yes, I know what you're going through, and I know how difficult it must be for you."

Somehow I had hit the jackpot! I had managed to stumble upon a way to bring up my negativity without being negative. As I sat there across from her, I couldn't believe my good fortune.

"I want to explain something to you I think will help," she began. "In life there is a 'penny in and a penny out' effect. For years you have been placing negative thoughts in your mind. Now you are beginning to place some positive thoughts in there. Think of it this way, before you can expect to see the results you desire, the negative penny you placed in your bank has to be removed and replaced with a positive one. Furthermore, you can only remove one penny at a time. And, as you are learning, it can be quite challenging to remove a negative penny from your bank. (I had a memory of a piggy bank I had as a kid. As it became fuller, it became harder for me to shake the money out of it. It could be a very frustrating process because I was always trying to get the money before the ice cream man's truck disappeared from my neighborhood. Talk about pressure!) Once you remove one negative penny, it becomes a little easier to remove the next. But it can only be accomplished one penny at a time. Then you can replace it with a positive penny. Again one at a time," she explained.

"The work of taking out the negative pennies and replacing them with positive ones takes time," June continued. "Turning your life around is a slow, step-by-step process. What you are calling bad luck is what a lot of people experience once they get by the initial excitement of trying to change their lives for the better. Bad luck has nothing to do with it. Bad luck is just the reality you have spent many years putting negative pennies into your bank. You have accumulated a lot of pennies. Now you have spent a few months improving your life but, just because you have removed a few negative pennies and maybe even replaced them with some positive ones, that doesn't mean that your bank is filled with positive pennies. You spent a lot of time becoming the person you were before you started working here. It will take you just as long to become the person you want to ultimately become. One penny at a time. One day at a time. That's how it works. As your thoughts and attitude slowly change, so will your results. That's how change works. That's how life works. And that is how a person truly grows in their career. Now you better get on the phones. It's a long race, and you can't quit until you cross the finish line!"

Even though I still owed a lot of money and had no signs that I was going to make any soon, I felt completely comforted by June's explanation. It all made sense (no pun intended) to me. Of course, change was going to take time. I had spent so many years going in one direction. It made sense to me at the beginning things wouldn't always start off so great. It takes awhile to get going. Of course, anything that can go wrong will, when you are starting something new. It all made sense to me.

I also realized there wasn't something fundamentally wrong with me. I wasn't damaged goods or a broke idiot, as I was given to thinking when things went wrong. June's talk made me feel good about myself again. I realized as powerful as she was in being able to cut to the core of my problems and the problems of the candidates, she was equally as gifted at being understanding and compassionate. Whatever she did, she did it with power. The joy she experienced while telling me about her ring, the times she had been frustrated with my negativity and stubbornness, the delight she took in talking to a candidate and the compassion she had just shown me were all done with a unique force. I had never experienced that kind of power. I didn't know it was possible. I had been in total despair before our conversation. Now I felt great. I had been terrified I was going to be out on the streets. Now I was sure a placement and the money it would provide was just around the corner. Before I was sure there was something wrong with me. Now I knew, with time, I could do anything I set my mind to. I had been furious at God for denying me. Now I was grateful He was helping me in such a big way. This was the effect of June's short talk with me.

It was also during these moments I would have a small insight into the magnitude of how lucky I was to be working for June. God had given me exactly what I had asked for – a mentor who could bring out the best in me, who would teach me to be honest and strong, who would know the worst about me but would lift me up anyway.

That day I got on the phone and had some great success in my marketing and recruiting calls. I was determined to shake a few negative pennies loose before this opportunity disappeared around the corner.

"Taker"

As the days went by my "penny in, penny out" talk with June kept my mind and emotions in a very positive place. When something went wrong, I was able to take it in stride. In my personal life, when another bill became due I didn't panic. I had it firmly in my mind that I was replacing my negative pennies, one cold call, one day of work at a time. I understood that my growth was going to be a marathon, not a sprint. And one day soon, I believed my financial situation would turn around.

June could sense the change in me as well. Our talks became less intense. Instead of June constantly working on me, we were beginning to work together. It was fun. We discussed the candidates I recruited at length, and I was continuing to learn from June's observations about their good decisions and their mistakes. Secretly I got a real kick out of talking about other peoples' problems. I was tired of my own issues and it felt good to talk about someone else's problems for a change. Okay, so I don't get points for that.

However, I knew I was growing. I felt as though I had overcome a big hurdle in learning how to stop taking everything so personally. I was able to think more clearly and enjoy the small victories I had in my recruiting and marketing efforts, not to mention in my personal life. For the first time I could remember, I felt I was standing on solid ground.

I sent out a candidate to one of my new clients, and the interview went well. The company was very interested in making my candidate an offer, and the candidate was equally excited about the position. I couldn't wait to get the call with the offer. I waited and waited and waited. Then they called. June wanted me to take the call in her office so she could hear me as I got my first placement. I sat there, pen in hand, ready to write down the salary information. Instead, the company was calling to let me know that the employee, who had given notice, had decided to stay with the company. I was so disappointed, I felt like I did when I was 10-years-old and someone had stolen my brand new bicycle. I took a few deep breaths, gathered my notebook and pen from June's desk and got back on the phone to make more calls.

About half an hour went by and June called me into her office. "Sit down, I want to talk to you," she began. I had already developed a kind of Pavlovian response to her requests. As the fear would begin to take over, my body would tense up. I would try to act normal so June would not be able to see how afraid I was. I started thinking of what I had done wrong and began to prepare for what was coming. "I didn't do it," was my old reaction. "Don't be defensive" was my new mantra. But no matter what was going through my mind, I knew I was about to be called out. Again.

"I was thinking you have been doing a pretty good job lately, but you just don't seem to be able to make a placement. With all the changes and challenges you have in your life, even if you do make a placement, I don't believe you will be able to make them on a consistent basis. You seem to be doing a good job of recruiting candidates and marketing to companies. I don't know if this is going to work, but I thought if we worked together you might be able to make it. I would place the candidates you recruit, and you would spend more time recruiting. Of course, when we make a placement you would get a much smaller portion of the commission than if you had made the placement on your own, but a smaller portion of something is better than a large portion of nothing," she concluded.

What was going on? For the second time in a row June had not called me out as I had expected! It had taken me months to finally learn how not to completely overreact to June's constructive criticism. Now that I had finally learned how not to fall apart, she wasn't calling me out! "How strange? How wonderfully strange!" I remembered thinking.

I had two reactions to June's proposal. The competitive side of me felt that I didn't want to give up on doing the job on my own. I didn't like seeing myself as the guy who needed help. On the other hand, I was really amazed and extremely excited June thought enough of me to want to work together. Moreover, I knew working with June meant I would make money. In a weird way it also meant that I had an invitation to legitimize my decision to work with her.

It really wasn't a difficult choice. Who was I kidding with my "I can do this on my own" attitude? I could play racquetball and basketball successfully on my own. I could drive a car, eat and breathe on my own. I could even fool people into thinking I had really accomplished something by graduating from college with double majors in highly intellectual fields. But I definitely could not make a placement. Making money was a subject in which I was failing miserably. I told June I thought it was a great idea, and we agreed on a new payment structure where I would receive a third of a normal commission on the placements where I recruited the candidate and another third if I brought in the client and June would work to close the placements.

"Now, once you make this choice, you can't go back on our deal. I don't want to keep changing the way we work. Do you understand that?" she asked. I assured her I understood what she was saying and, as of that day, our new arrangement went into effect.

I got busy in my new role. Now I was not only recruiting candidates for her clients, but I was also marketing her candidates to new companies. Working more closely together had a different feel to it. June's clients were much easier to recruit for because they were more established, high-quality companies. Her candidates were a lot easier to market, as well. Many of them had worked with June in the past. They were not only more marketable than my candidates; they were also much more committed to working with June than my candidates had been with me.

Our end-of-the-day talks began to take on a different mood as well. June started asking me questions about my life in Santa Cruz. She laughed when she discovered I was bringing tofu sandwiches to work every day. (I'm talking about an uncontrollable, whole-body shaking "help me, I can't breathe" laugh that lasted for a good half an hour.) She was fascinated that I didn't know how to dress professionally. ("Didn't anyone teach you how to dress properly?") She was flabbergasted to hear what they had taught me at the university. ("How can a school teach you Capitalism is a bad thing and Marxism is good?" "How could the school authorities allow kids to use drugs right under their noses?" "What do you mean the women would take their tops off during outdoor classes?" "Wasn't there any kind of morality?") These were just some of the issues we would discuss. The more we talked, the more I was beginning to see things from June's perspective. I was starting to realize just how strange my world had become living in Santa Cruz.

As our relationship continued to grow stronger I found myself turning to June for advice on just about everything. Every day, her schedule permitting, I visited her office and asked her question after question. "What should I work on today?" "What did you think of that last candidate?" "What should I do about my friend who is so negative?" "How do I handle the personal calls I'm getting from the collection agencies?" I asked her advice about everything and anything I could think of. And even though she was very busy running a business and closing placements, she took the time to talk to me and help with whatever issue was on my mind.

Then one day June asked me to come see her in her office. This time I wasn't the least bit apprehensive. I felt so good about our new arrangement and the direction it had taken our working relationship that all my fear of being called out had completely disappeared. "What's up?" I asked her enthusiastically.

"I want to talk to you," she began. Something wasn't right, I could sense it. My body went into hyper-overdrive, becoming more rigid, as I tried to prepare for what was coming next. "It occurs to me our talks are all one way. I'm helping you while taking time away from my work, and you don't do anything in return."

She continued, but I tuned her out. I didn't want to hear it. She stopped for a moment and I realized that I was no longer looking at her. I was staring at my knees. "Look up at me. I enjoy helping you. I really do, and you are making some progress. But I believe I could help you until the end of time, and it would never occur to you to give something back in return. You are a TAKER. You take without a thought of giving," she concluded.

"You're a taker." I was crushed. "You're a taker." Suddenly making a placement meant absolutely nothing to me. "You're a taker." June's comment shook me. Just like her comment, "You're a liar," during our initial interview. It went right to my core. I felt completely and utterly exposed, humiliated and embarrassed.

I made a few feeble attempts to defend myself. Ironically, most of them were lies. I tried explaining I was going to do something for her; I just didn't know what to do. I tried to tell her she was making a big assumption about me without really knowing me well enough. I tried several other defenses, most of them too ridiculous to even remember. But I knew she was right.

Once I could admit June was right about me, a funny thing happened. Although I had worked very hard to have people see me as a nice guy and I really hated being called out as a taker, a part of me felt relieved. Like a criminal running from the law, there is a certain degree of relief when you realize you have finally been caught. I came around and stopped defending myself. Would I have thought to do something in exchange for all the extra help June was giving me? The answer, if I was really honest about it, was 'no.' I was so needy. I felt I somehow deserved and was entitled to everything she was giving me. She was right; it would not had occurred to me to do something for her in exchange for all the extra help she was giving me in my personal and professional life. I was a taker.

"You will never learn to feel better about yourself until you learn how to give of yourself," she continued. "You are a taker like your father. The basis of a healthy relationship, professional or personal, is the ability to learn how to give and take. If all you know is how to take, you will never be in a healthy relationship. On the other hand, if all I knew was how to give, I would never be in one either. The key is to learn how to do both. I really don't know how you could get to be 23 years old and not know how to give, but if you're going to continue to work for me, you better start learning. I'm not going to work with a taker. I don't care how much I like you," she said.

It took everything I had not to feel sorry for myself. I was trying to listen and think clearly as June was talking to me. I was thinking of everything I had told myself about not reacting. I was trying so hard to really take it in. "So what can I do to learn how to be a giver?" I asked sheepishly.

June stopped and thought about my question. "Well", she began, "I need my garage cleaned. It's a mess. You could start there."

The Mop Is Your Friend

I woke up the next Saturday morning and headed over to June's house to begin my transformation from being a "taker" to whatever it was I was supposed to be ("fair" was my best guess, but it was just a guess). It was an especially beautiful morning, and the thought of spending the day indoors cleaning a garage did not appeal to me at all. I knew, however, if I were to keep the peace with June, I had better be on time and do a good job. Still, I couldn't help but think about all the fun things I could be doing if I hadn't told June that I would help her.

When I arrived at June's house, she was in her usual, upbeat mood. She was glad to see me. We talked briefly until it was time to get to work. June showed me her garage. Half of it was perfectly organized and clean. The other half looked like a bomb had gone off in a furniture consignment store. It was a total mess.

June asked me to find her a folding chair so she could sit down while she helped me sort out the garage. She told me while I was cleaning she would go through her boxes and decide what she wanted to keep and what she would throw away. I looked at a pile of twenty or more boxes in one corner of the garage alone. "I'm a bit of a pack rat, I'm afraid," she said with a laugh. "But I absolutely love being organized. That's my fantasy. One day I will have everything in my home and at the office completely organized."

June instructed me on how to get started. She asked me to get everything out of the garage so that I could sweep and mop the floor. As I began taking each item out of the garage, I found myself enjoying the work. There was something about being around June that made me feel good about myself. I remember thinking perhaps this give and take thing she was talking about wasn't going to be as bad as I had thought.

After some time, some real progress was made in clearing out the mess. I started playing a game with myself to see how fast I could get everything out. The faster I worked, I reasoned, the sooner I could go and enjoy the day.

On one of my trips back from the driveway, I noticed June was working on the same box I had given her over an hour ago. She hadn't thrown away one object! She would pull an item out of the box, look at it for awhile, then very carefully put it right back. As I watched her, it occurred to me that at her current pace, I could be stuck helping her for the next 20 years!

After several hours, I had everything out of the garage and was ready to begin sweeping the floors. I was still playing my game of seeing how fast I could finish. Then I caught what appeared to be a huge break. Because of her poor health, June was running out of energy and got up from her chair. She lay down for awhile and she instructed me to come in and get her when I was finished.

I swept the floors and began the process of putting everything back. I had been working for almost three hours. My thoughts began to shift from "how fast can I get this job completed?" to "why am I doing this job in the first place?" I was missing out on a great day. I didn't know anyone else who would be willing to spend their Saturday cleaning out their boss's garage. Then I thoughts about June in her house resting. If she didn't have the energy to help with her own garage, why should I be out here? I had said I would help, but this was unfair. In fact, it was ridiculous!

I put everything back in the garage as quickly as I could. I also reorganized the garage to look more presentable. Once I was finished, I went inside to fetch June.

I found her sleeping on her couch. I awoke her and announced I finished the garage. She looked shocked and asked me for the time. When I told her, she looked even further surprised. She stared at me as if I had awakened her from a nap she had anticipated should have been much longer. "You can't possibly be finished," she said. Thinking about how my how-fast-can-I-go game had really sped up my work. I assured her I was finished and helped her off the sofa.

"Let's take a look," she said.

When we got to the garage June looked around and asked me, "Did you mop the floors with soap and water?"

"No" I replied. "I've never heard of anyone washing their garage floors with soap and water."

"You've got to wash them or the floor is not clean," she said.

"June, trust me, NOBODY washes their garage floors! I swept them and besides, I've been here for more than three hours and it's my weekend… fine, I'll wash the floors if that's what you want," I said in frustration.

I started hauling boxes out of the garage when I heard June say, "Go ahead and go. If you don't want to do the job correctly, I don't want you to be here. Now, go."

I looked up at her and saw she had gone from being half asleep to wide awake. Her eyes had grown very dark. I felt myself shrinking smaller as her five-foot frame seemed to, supernaturally, grow larger.

My mind began to race: She has no right to be upset. I did what I said I would do. I cleaned her garage. Who has ever heard of washing a garage floor with soap and water? She couldn't even get through one box. Where does she get off getting mad at me? Why should I be doing this in the first place? My family and friends were right. She's taking advantage of me!

Later that afternoon, my sense of justification began to give way to an all too familiar sick feeling in the pit of my stomach. New thoughts began to make their way into my mind: June has done so much to help me. What's so bad about wanting to have your garage floors mopped with soap? And here's the big one, June has taken so much of her personal time to help me with my problems. This was my chance to help her, and all I did is end up getting mad at her!

With my confession came a new set of thoughts. Suddenly, I was remembering all the time and effort June had taken to help me without ever complaining. I felt ashamed of myself for acting so petty.

Of course, the rest of my precious weekend was ruined. The garage cleaning episode had shown me exactly what June meant about me being a taker. I hadn't been aware of it before. Not really. Now I could see the inequity of my idea about giving and receiving. Giving did not come naturally to me. It was a forced act. I could give in short bursts, but even that was on my terms.

June gave in a manner I had never experienced before. Where people like my favorite teachers had been gentle and inviting in their giving, June was strong, results oriented and had the ability to dig deep to the core of what was really wrong with me. Because she was able to see my problems so clearly, she was able to help me where I needed it most. When June helped someone, she gave everything she had. She was able to clear her mind and focus all her thoughts and energies on a person's most important needs, desires and wounds. As she was doing with me, she was able to see into people and tell them exactly what they needed to hear for them to move forward in their lives. She had done all this for me, and I hadn't been able to find it in myself to honor her simple request. I hadn't washed her garage floors.

Monday morning I went into June's office and sincerely apologized for my poor attitude. I explained to her I had given it a lot of thought (this time, it was true) and I had come to realize I really wanted to learn how to give. I told her if she would give me a second chance, I would guarantee her she would have the cleanest, most organized garage in all of California. Despite her obvious frustration with me, I had made her the one offer she couldn't refuse – the possibility of a clean and organized garage. She reluctantly agreed to give me another chance.

"Let me tell you something that will help you. Whenever you find yourself feeling justified about an issue, any issue, you can bet you're wrong," she said. "The fact you felt so justified about not cleaning the floors should have told you something was off in you. Whenever I find myself feeling justified, I know I'm off – I'm not being entirely honest with myself. For example, I could have felt justified in being upset you were in such a rush to finish the job Saturday, but I know you don't understand how to give of yourself. I took that into account and saved myself a lot of heartache, although I was very disappointed in you," she concluded.

I hadn't realized she had picked up that I was in a rush to finish her job. I thought I had hidden that from her. No wonder she wanted me to leave that day. She knew I didn't really want to be there in the first place. I felt very lucky I was being given another chance.

As I left her office feeling good about my small victory, I couldn't help but laugh at how interesting my life with June had become. Who would believe feeling great because my boss had agreed to give me another opportunity to clean her garage floor?

"This sure isn't a normal job," I thought.

Attitude Shift

That next Saturday I pulled up to June's house, determined to give her garage everything I had. I immediately went to work pulling out all the boxes and objects I had pulled out the week before and began placing them on the driveway. After several hours of lugging everything out of the garage, I was ready to begin washing the floors with soap, water and a mop. I scrubbed for over an hour until I felt June would be happy with my results. Unlike the previous week, I wasn't working hard in order to leave as soon as I could. I was working to please June. I wanted to give her the clean, organized garage she had asked me for in the first place.

And the funny thing was, I found myself really enjoying it, not just for a few moments at a time as was the case the previous week. I was really into it. The idea of pleasing June had me genuinely focused, motivated and in a surprisingly great mood. I must have looked a little ridiculous getting down on my hands and knees scrubbing grease stains, but I didn't care. I was determined to deliver on my promise.

After three sweepings, two thorough washings, and a complete wall cleaning (including the removal of some pretty serious spider webs) I invited June to come and inspect my work. She entered the garage and took inventory. When she had looked everything over, her eyes lit up.

"This is great. It really looks fantastic," she said.

A sense of pride came over my whole body. It felt great. The look of utter delight I saw on June's face had a profound effect on me. I had made her happy. I had given her something she enjoyed without asking or expecting anything in return. This was what it meant to give – to really give unconditionally. The feeling of pride and joy I was experiencing was amazing. Unlike the awful sick, pit-of-my-stomach feeling that came whenever I took without giving, this was a sensation I knew I wanted to experience again. And all I had to do was to give back. It was simple.

As I stood there enjoying myself, June said, "Let me ask you, just for kicks, what if we moved the boxes from the right-hand side over to the left to see if we could make more room in here?"

That doesn't even make sense, was my first thought. *What are you talking about? If you put them on the other side they will take up just as much room,* was my second thought. I could feel my good attitude getting ready to leave the garage. I told myself not to react. After what seemed like an eternity, but was actually just a matter of seconds, I could feel myself beginning to calm down. I then thought: "If June wants the boxes on the other side of her garage, then that's what I'm going to do."

"Well, let's move them over and find out" were the words that came out of my mouth.

I forced myself not to think of all the work I had just done for her. I refused to allow myself to ponder just how ridiculous her request was. I would not let myself think of the time I had already put into the job and how much more it was going to take to honor June's "just for kicks" request. Instead, I got busy moving the boxes. *This is a test,* I told myself, *to see if I will crack under pressure, and I'm not going to lose it. I will find a way to have a good attitude.*

The test became even harder when June decided to stay in the garage and tell me exactly where she wanted each box to be moved. She seemed to be operating from some grand scheme of organization only she could understand. Boxes that had been placed together were now being separated into different sections. Occasionally, I would stand there for a minute or two longer holding a heavy box while she thought about where she wanted it to go. The whole thing seemed absurd, but I just kept thinking, *I'm not going to let this get to me. I'm going to do a great job.*

Suddenly she looked up at me and saw the look of strain on my face. As if she was seeing the absurdity of the situation for the first time, she burst out laughing. As soon as I saw her laugh, I started laughing just as hard. Neither one of us could stop. I had to put the box down before I dropped it. And we just kept laughing.

Finally, we both caught our breath. June got a tissue to wipe away her tears, and we resumed working. This time June didn't care where the boxes went. "Just put them anywhere you like," she said.

We talked and had a great afternoon as I finished moving the final boxes. When I was finished, she invited me inside her home, fixed me something to eat and told me a few of her stories. Oddly, it was a great afternoon.

As I got ready to leave, I took another look at the work I had done in June's garage. It really did look fantastic. Her garage looked new and clean. I realized that I didn't just feel good about giving back to June.

I felt good about the work I had done. It was only a garage, but it was made better because of my hard work.

As I got in my car and took one last look, I noticed something very strange. The garage appeared to have a lot more space in it. Somehow, mysteriously, the garage seemed much bigger with the boxes moved from one side to the other.

I could have sat there and tried to figure out the mystery, but instead I just laughed and headed home. It had been a great day.

Carolyn's Big Chance

Be Where You are Going

After interviewing Carolyn, June had determined she was a good match for the Human Resource opening I had been recruiting. June felt Carolyn had "found her backbone" and had not only taken responsibility for her own weaknesses (instead of blaming her boss for them), but was now seeing the opportunity to grow from the adversity she was currently facing.

June did an amazing job of presenting Carolyn to my new client. She spoke honestly about Carolyn's strengths and weaknesses. When June believed in a candidate, she had a way of describing their shortcomings in a manner that didn't sound like a negative at all. June's enthusiasm for candidates had the effect of neutralizing her very forthright description of their negatives. Her genuine confidence in and excitement about Carolyn left the client spellbound. If the client could have put words to this reaction it might be, "I have to meet this fascinating person you're describing." Only June could get that reaction and, at the same time, be totally upfront about the candidate's shortcomings.

Carolyn arrived at our offices an hour before her interview for her send-out. June prepared her for the interview by going over the importance of being her best self. She coached Carolyn in how to be focused, enthusiastic, comfortable and confident.

"Bringing your best self to an interview is a similar experience to trying on an evening gown for the first time. At first, it feels unnatural. That sense of 'this is not the real me.' But wait 10 to 15 minutes and, for most people, something very interesting happens. They begin to feel comfortable. And surprisingly, it doesn't take very long for a complete transformation to take place. We go from the 'this just isn't the real me' stage to the 'wow, this is the real me' stage very quickly. In fact, some people go from the 'this isn't me' stage' to the 'wow, this is the real me' to the 'this is not only the real me, but do you have an even more elegant dress?' stage in record time. When it comes to jewelry, I believe I personally hold the record!" June said laughing.

"I think I'd fall into that last category myself. I have no problem upgrading when it comes to the finer things in life. My 'this isn't the real me' stage lasts only about a nanosecond!" Carolyn said joining in June's laughter.

I was sitting there in my typical uptight manner, but when I saw the two of them laughing I couldn't help laughing myself. It's not I thought anything June said was funny, but watching her laugh, I couldn't help but crack up. When June laughed not only did her whole face light up, but her whole body shook. The look of complete and utter joy was a sight to behold. She laughed, as she did everything else, with uninhibited abandonment.

Collecting herself, June continued. "That's what you want to do in an interview – try on your best self. Bring your most confident, prepared, relaxed self. At first it won't feel natural. However, like the dress, you will soon not only get used to it, you will grow to enjoy it. You may even find yourself wanting more. This is one of the keys of growing in your career. You have to BE where you're going."

"I'm not sure I completely understand what you mean by that," Carolyn said.

I had to admit that I, too, had absolutely NO idea what June meant.

"To grow in your career you must have a vision for who you want to become ultimately – a clear sense of how you would feel if you were actually living in your dream career. It's not a vision of WHAT you are doing. It's a vision of WHO you are, meaning your inner sense of confidence, pride and fulfillment. It's not about money, status or what other people think of you. It's your dream of who you would like to be ultimately. Again, it's important that you keep this completely separate from the dream you may have of your material success. Once you form a clear sense of who you dream of becoming, you bring that 'you' to the interview," June explained.

I was having one of those rare moments where June was explaining something important, and I actually felt that I understood her. Unfortunately, when I looked over at Carolyn she looked completely confused. June must have noticed Carolyn's expression as well, but it didn't seem to stop her from continuing to make her point.

"Bringing your best self to the interview is also critical to making a good decision about a job offer. Good decision making is far more intuitive than analytical. When you bring your highest expectations concerning the feel of the environment to the interview, your instincts will speak loud and clear. The feel of the environment always reflects the qualities of the leadership. It feels good to be in the environment of a company where the leadership is involved, has integrity, purpose and a great vision for its future. It doesn't feel good to be in an environment with leadership that is cold, indifferent, not entirely honest, and lacks any meaningful purpose in its mission. When you focus on money, title, promises of growth, or responsibilities, you miss out on the subtleties of how the environment feels to you. The feeling is there, but you are not paying enough attention to it. That's the analytical approach most people take to interviewing and decision making. The key is to bring your best self to the interview and get your mind off your fears and concerns. If you walk out of the interview and you still have a good percentage of that feeling remaining, then you know you have come upon a great opportunity. If most of that feeling is gone, I suggest you run – don't walk away from the job."

"June, that's a lot to take in during 45 minutes or so."

"Why?" June shot back.

"Well, for one thing I don't know anything about the people yet. They may not be the kind of people I want to work for."

"What are you afraid of," June asked.

The feeling in the room was taking a strange turn. The three of us had been laughing just moments earlier, but now there was that weird sense I felt every time I was about to experience June's professional wrath.

"Nothing, really, I just want to meet them before I get my hopes up. That's not unusual," Carolyn said.

"No, it's not unusual, but it is a foolish approach to interviewing. Frankly, I find it cowardly," June said.

I could see Carolyn was getting very upset just as she had the first time she had interviewed with June.

"I don't think I'm a coward," she said defensively.

"Listen, if you approach this interview with fear, all you're going to accomplish is one of two things: if the company happens to be great, your hesitation will turn them off and you will not get an offer you desire. Or your fear will lead you to being more analytical and less intuitive which will only result in you being more easily manipulated," June said.

"I don't understand."

"When we live in fear, we attract exactly what we are afraid of. You, for instance, are afraid you are going to be passive again and not listen to your instincts when things go wrong. You would love to find a company that would reassure you they will treat you well. That would feel wonderful, to have someone look you in the eyes and say 'Carolyn, we will not lie to you or let you down,' June said.

"Okay, what's wrong with wanting to hear that?"

"Nothing is wrong with wanting to hear it, but everything is wrong with needing to. How easy would it be for someone to say those words to you and not mean a word of it?" June asked.

"I don't know, I guess it would be pretty easy," she replied.

"Well let me tell you, it would be remarkably easy for any company to say those words to you. Any company, from the very worst to the very best, can say those words because they are just words. Words don't mean a thing. And that's exactly what happens when a person like you hasn't processed their fears and taken responsibility for their own poor decisions. You don't trust yourself, so you need reassurance from others. And guess what kind of companies tend to do a lot of verbal reassuring in their interviews?" June asked.

"I can answer that," I piped in. "Before working here, I worked for a company that promised me I could make a lot of money. Because I needed money so badly and was afraid I didn't know how to make it, it felt great to have someone sit across from me in an interview and tell me I could make a lot of it. The thing is, I wasn't paying attention to any of the other clues that were taking place in the interview."

"Like what?" Carolyn asked.

"Like that the guy wasn't asking me much about my skills and experience. Or that he seemed very anxious and nervous. Or that he, when I really think back on it, didn't seem up front or honest. There were so many clues it was going to be a bad experience, but I didn't pay attention because I was so afraid of not having money," I explained.

"What happened to the job?"

"I worked really hard and ended up earning the money I so desperately needed. The only problem was the company was being run by a couple of thieves. They left town with all the company's profits, and I never saw a dime of what I had earned. It left me more afraid and desperate than ever. That's what June is trying to tell you about what fears do to us," I said.

"How was it when you interviewed with June," she asked.

"It was a completely different experience. She wanted to know what kind of person I was. She asked me questions no one had ever asked me before. I could tell she really cared about her company. I could also tell that, unlike the last guy who hired me, she was honest. She didn't promise me a lot of money either. In fact, she told me making money here would take quite a while and involve a lot of hard work and commitment," I said.

"And believe me he was not what I was looking for," June said. "He didn't know how to be honest with himself, his clothes were awful, and he had gone to school at the University of Santa Cruz, which I think so little of. There really wasn't anything attractive about him. But I got a sense he cared and, for some reason, I hired him," June explained.

Now it was my turn to feel defensive. For the first time in an interview I had actually felt that I had been contributing. I was opening up about my mistakes and about what I was learning. For all of about three seconds, I had felt really good about myself. Then June had to tell her about my shortcomings, and my good feeling was gone. Gone far away.

Despite my defensive reaction, I saw that Carolyn's face was beginning to soften. "I just don't want to make the same mistake. I don't want to end up working for someone like my current manager. You're right. I am afraid I'm going to make the same mistake."

"Do you really believe that is what I want for you?" June asked.

"No, I can tell you are trying to help me, June. I appreciate what you are doing."

"The only way you are going to find a company where the leadership has 'backbone,' as you called it, is to get focused on looking for quality in the interview. You can't possibly get focused on something you're afraid doesn't exist. You have to start by convincing yourself there are companies out there where leadership has the backbone you are looking for. If you don't believe what you want is out there, you might as well give up your search now and stay where you are. I can tell you right now you are not going to find what you are not sure exists," June explained.

"I hadn't looked at it that way. You're right. I think I've just gotten so used to my current boss that I've given up on believing there are truly good companies to work for."

"That's because you still haven't taken responsibility for your part in this. You see yourself as a victim. But did anyone tell you that you had to continue to work for someone you didn't respect? Did anyone twist your arm and make you stay in an environment where you were being ridiculed?" June asked.

"No" Carolyn replied.

"You made the choice to stay. You had the power to leave the moment your instincts told you that things were very wrong in your company. You chose not to use that power. The moment you made that choice, you became a victim. Now after a year and a half you can't take the situation anymore, but you have grown so accustomed to giving up your power, you've come to believe you can't have what you want."

"You're right, June. That is how I feel."

"Well, let me assure you that you still have your power. But if you're going to rediscover it, you had better start by being more honest with yourself about the role you played in your current job" June said.

For what seemed like several minutes, Carolyn didn't say anything. She just sat there staring into space. It seemed to me she was replaying her current work situation in her mind. I could see she was really thinking about what June was saying.

"I did choose to stay," Carolyn said slowly, as if just coming to the realization for the first time. "I should have begun looking for a new job the moment I realized that my boss was afraid to confront the troublemakers. The funny thing is I knew it. I knew I had to leave. You're right. I do need to be more honest about that. I could have left anytime I wanted. I'm the one who was afraid to do anything about my problems. I kept putting it on my boss but, as you keep pointing out, it's really me I've been mad at and disappointed in, not my boss."

"I want you to imagine you had decided to leave the company the moment you knew you should have. Can you imagine that for a moment?"

"Yes, it's a good image!" Carolyn responded.

"Now, let's imagine you were taking that 'Carolyn' out to this interview. How would she be different from the Carolyn I see now?"

"Wow, she's completely different! She's confident. She's not so afraid and timid. She knows exactly what she wants. I see what you're getting at, June."

"Now you've got it!" June replied.

"I can't believe how much of myself I've lost. A moment ago when you said I've lost my power, I had no idea what you were talking about. But, you're right, that's exactly it. I've lost my confidence. No, to be completely honest, I think I've given it away."

"Yes, that's right. You have given it away. Now don't you think it's time to take it back?"

The rest of the send-out was amazing. Carolyn was a new woman. She was no longer the scared, insecure candidate sitting across from me just a few moments before. She had become totally alive. She was no longer afraid of making a mistake. She no longer had the need to be reassured. Instead, she was confident, focused, enthusiastic, relaxed and very excited about the interview. She decided to bring her best self, and she was free to do so. She was going to approach the interview under the assumption it was going to be the opportunity of a lifetime and the leadership was strong with plenty of backbone to back her up in difficult situations. She was also confident if for any reason the leadership lacked what she was looking for, then she would be able to discern the situation accurately. She was no longer looking for reassurance. Rather, she was looking inward – to her own instincts and intuitions about the integrity of the leadership. She was using her power to discern if the leadership of the company would respect her and back her up in difficult situations.

It was interesting to me how she had gone from being so afraid to being so confident. I had thought this was a send out gone wrong. Instead of talking about the client and what they were looking for, we were spending all our time going over many of the same issues addressed in Carolyn's initial interview. But somehow June had managed to get Carolyn focused, enthusiastic and relaxed without talking about the position at all. By releasing Carolyn from her fear, June had given Carolyn the ability to discern the right match from a poor match. In addition, she had managed to make her far more attractive to a company with good leadership.

Even from my underdeveloped emotional state I could see, without June's help, Carolyn would have been destined to repeat her mistake. I was seeing this horrible cycle moving through the careers of most of the candidates we interviewed. Their first job usually was a pretty good one. That's the job they took because the people or the company seemed "pretty cool" or "fun" or "interesting." They were choosing jobs mostly on their intuitive feel for the people in the company. But then as their careers progressed into their second or third job, things would begin to go sideways. Those were the jobs people usually accepted because "it was in my field" or "the money was right" or "it looks good on my résumé" or "there was the opportunity to grow." Typically, in the second or third jobs people began to accept positions, not on the basis of how the job felt but on what they thought the job could do for them. The intuitive approach to decision making was being replaced by an analytical one. And the reality was, no matter what a job could do FOR a person, it was what the job did TO the person that ended up being the overriding issue in each career.

That's where June came in. She was interested in the inner person, the real person. I sat there in her office watching as she set one candidate after another free from the cycle of dissatisfaction that had enveloped their career. She was reorienting them, restoring them, delivering them out of fear and resignation and giving them back their confidence and their ability to discern and attract a job that would reflect the best in them.

As I drove home that evening, I found myself pondering what it would be like to go through life the way June prepared her candidates for a send out. How would my world be different if I woke up every day thinking that this was going to be the best day of my life? What would it be like to bring my *best self* to each day? The first thought that went through my mind was, *given my life, I would end up feeling disappointed a lot*. I laughed as I realized that had been Carolyn's answer: "I don't want to get my hopes up only to end up disappointed." When she responded that way to June, I immediately saw how she was protecting herself. Because I wanted her to do well in her interview, it was easy for me to see the fear in her reaction. Now that it was my turn for some self-examination, it wasn't so easy to see my own underlying fear.

The next thoughts that entered my mind were: *It wouldn't cost me anything to bring my best self to each new day. What if I came into work each day expecting to recruit a great candidate? What if I expected to help make two or three placements a week? What if I expected my finances to turn around? What if I expected my marriage to be more fulfilling?*

As I asked myself each question, I could feel myself becoming more alive and confident. It felt as though I had just plugged myself into some mysterious energy source. I could see myself accomplishing everything I wanted. I felt strong. It wasn't that I suddenly believed bad things were never going to happen to me again. I no longer was afraid of them happening. From this mindset, I somehow knew for certain bad things weren't going to stop me from accomplishing what I set my mind to do.

For the next half hour of my commute home and for the first time in my life, I knew what it was like to think and live without fear. This new-found confidence was leading me to have one epiphany after another. Of course, in actuality, my epiphanies were nothing more than the exact concepts I had been hearing June tell our candidates for months. But it felt as though I, alone, was discovering these great truths.

Fear was blocking me from living the life I really desired. Fear was preventing me from being the person I wanted to be. Fear had led me to make bad decisions. Conversely, it had been courage that had brought me to June and courage had allowed me not to leave when things got tough. Bringing my best self to my life really meant overcoming fear and living with courage. Who was it that said, "Courage is moving forward in the face of fear?"

Fear was also responsible for distorting my perceptions. That truth not only applied to me but also explained why so many candidates were choosing bad companies to work for. I wondered if their personal lives reflected their work lives. Carolyn's fear had the effect of limiting her ability to perceive and discern what was happening beneath the surface. Her fear of not being supported created the need to be reassured. The companies that did a lot of reassuring also tended to be companies that lacked integrity. That's what created that awful cycle of taking one bad job after another. Fear was self-fulfilling.

Courage, too, had self-fulfilling consequences. The more candidates believed their deepest desires would be met; the more likely it was to happen. The candidates who had the courage to overcome their fears were the same ones who were able to discern the great companies from the others. When I acted with courage, I saw how June was doing everything she could to help me grow. When I acted with fear, I was certain she was out to make my life even worse than it already was. My state of mind determined my ability to perceive a situation accurately. Because my state of mind was critical to my ability to perceive, it was also critical to my ability to make a good decision. This was not only true for me, but it was true for the candidates, as well. That's why June spent so much of her time helping candidates identify and overcome their fears.

At the heart of it all, I thought, *a person's career is a self-fulfilling prophecy. You must know yourself to understand what is happening to you and why it's happening.*

As I pulled up to my driveway, I had one more epiphany. Since we are all creatures of fear and fear is what stands between us and our fulfillment, the most important decision a person could make in their career is to work for leadership who has courage. That leadership would challenge them on their fears and limitations. Before I could lose the thought I took out a pad and scribbled on a piece of paper: "We all need a business environment where we can grow in our inner world so that we can understand ourselves better. Then we can grow toward becoming the person we are capable of becoming. The desire to become the person we are capable of becoming, our 'best self, is the underlying secret desire of everyone's career. That is true for all of us whether we are aware of it or not."

By spotting trends in a résumé and by asking a series of intelligent questions, June pinpointed candidates' deepest desires even if they could not or would not articulate them. That was why June was working so hard to help get our best candidates into companies with strong leadership. It was also the reason she tried so hard to communicate the importance of working for good leadership to the candidates she knew we were not going to place. She knew this simple truth was what people needed to know most. If she could make a placement – great. If she could give her best to a stranger even without making a placement – that would do too.

"For such as smart woman, you sure can be dense."
June Gregory

Triumph

June had asked Carolyn to return to our office after her interview. I was so excited about a possible placement I couldn't concentrate. Unable to work, the only thing I could manage to do was to pretend to make recruiting calls while I waited for her return. Pretending to make calls was a lot of work. I had to spend time looking at all the phone numbers on my list. I had to pretend that looking at the numbers had some kind of purpose (as if one random number was somehow better than another). I had to hope that June wouldn't notice I wasn't actually on the phone. Occasionally, I had to pick the phone up and dial, hoping no one would answer. If they did answer, I had to pretend I cared about what I was doing, and so on. Somewhere along the way, it occurred to me that recruiting in earnest was a whole lot easier than faking it.

Finally, after several hours, Carolyn returned. The three of us gathered in June's office.

"How did it go?" June asked her eyes full of life.

"June it was incredible! I loved it. You were right, the people were amazing. The moment I walked in, I could tell it was a great place to work. The physical environment is a lot less attractive than I'm used to, but the feeling there is so positive and upbeat! The first thing I noticed was the receptionist had a big smile on her face. Crystal, the office manager who is leaving, came out to greet me. She was great too. She made me feel comfortable right away. It didn't feel like I was in an interview. It just felt like we were talking as friends, but we were able to find out a lot about one another. And I learned a lot about what they were looking for," she explained.

Looking at Carolyn, she really did seem like a new person. She was even more relaxed and confident than she had been when she left our office for the interview. She was shining. More than just confident and relaxed, she seemed to be at peace with herself. It was as though some great burden had been taken from her. She wasn't the same woman we had been talking with just a couple of hours ago.

"The moment I started talking with them I could tell they were a great company," I said. I wanted the placement so badly I would have said anything to reinforce Carolyn's interest in the position. The funny thing was I really did believe what I was saying.

"What did they ask you?" June asked Carolyn.

"They asked me to tell them about myself. Everything just flowed. I told them about my current job and about two of my previous positions. You would have been proud of me. I was focused on telling them about the things I had accomplished that were exactly what they needed. They asked me my reasons for leaving each company and what I was looking for in my next position. I know they asked some other questions but, to be honest, I don't remember what they were. The conversation was so natural."

"Who, besides Crystal, did you meet with?" June asked.

"Things went so well with Crystal that she wanted me to meet the President. His name was Tom. I don't remember his last name. He gave me his card if you need it."

June looked at his card and wrote down his last name. "What did you think of him?" June asked enthusiastically.

"Oh, he was great!" she replied. "He was very down to earth and easy to talk to. He asked me my reasons for leaving my current company. I'm so appreciative you and I went over that so thoroughly before the interview. You were right, I would have blown it. He was very sharp. I felt like he was looking right through me. He would have picked up on a phony, superficial answer, and he would not have respected it."

"What did you say about your reasons for leaving?" June asked.

I could feel my body begin to tense, hoping that she got it right.

"I told him that I felt I had outgrown the position. I explained my boss had done a lot for me in my career. I told him he had the faith in me to promote me to the Human Resource Manager position and to give me the freedom to improve the department. At the beginning, things were great. But as time went on, I had realized my boss did not like to deal with conflict, and that quality made my job very difficult."

"How did he respond to your answer?" June asked.

"He was really good! He completely understood. He asked me to give him some examples. When I did, he nodded his head, and then he told me about a similar situation he had been in earlier in his career. We both ended up having a good laugh over how some individuals are just not born to manage other people," she said.

"Do you have any concerns about his management style or his ability to handle conflict?" June asked.

"Are you kidding? No, none at all. I think I could learn a lot from him. I'd love to work there."

The same woman who was so unsure of her ability to discern the quality of leadership based on a single interview was now sitting back in her chair without a worry in the world, saying in essence, "Are you kidding, of course I could tell. Anyone could!"

"Do you have any concerns or negatives?" June pressed.

Carolyn thought for a moment. "No, I really don't, June. It's funny but when I woke up this morning I told myself I was going to interview at least three or four companies before I made any decision. But I can honestly tell you if they made me an offer, I would take it in a heartbeat."

"Did you talk about money and benefits?" June asked.

"Yes, he asked me about what I was looking for, and I did exactly what you told me to do. I told him what I was making now and I'd like a step up. However, it was far more important to me to find the right position with the right company."

"How did he respond?"

"He really seemed to like my answer. He explained to me they don't necessarily pay the highest salary initially. But they were very generous with bonuses, and they were very good at rewarding their people financially over time. It turns out most of their employees have been working there a long time. This position is only open because Crystal is moving with her husband outside the area."

In what I was discovering to be typical June fashion, the conversation somehow went from talking about the interview to a discussion about jewelry. June appeared to have gotten all the information about the interview she needed. The two of them were having the time of their lives talking about rings, bracelets and other items I could care less about. I excused myself and left the room.

I don't think either of them noticed that I had left. They talked for another 20 minutes before I heard Carolyn leaving June's office. June told her she would be contacting the company and getting back to her as soon as possible.

As Carolyn left the office, I was right back at June's desk.

"What are you going to do next?" I asked anxiously.

"I want to call the company and get their feedback. You can stay and listen if you want."

I know I was there to learn how to follow up with a client, but my mind was not in a learning mode. My only concern was: Is this a placement? I wanted it so badly it hurt! I needed the money desperately, but more than that, I needed the validation I was on the right track. My fear I had made a foolish decision working for June was constantly haunting me. Being paid on commission was constantly preying on my insecurities. I knew without a doubt, June was helping me grow emotionally. I knew he was the answer to my prayer. What I didn't know was if I was supposed to be combining my desire to grow emotionally with my need to make money. No one in my life, other than June herself, understood why I was working for her without a salary to show for it.

My desire for Carolyn to get the offer went right to the core of the question I was subconsciously always asking myself: Can my financial and emotional need to grow be met in my work life? I had these deep core beliefs that said: Your work life is about making money. It's about survival and about security. It is not about emotional growth and fulfillment.

I don't even know where these beliefs were derived. Sometimes I would try to figure out where my assumptions had originated about my work life. I could remember seeing my Dad go to work every day as though he was going off to some secret world I wasn't supposed to know anything about. He rarely talked about his work. I could also remember overhearing an argument between my dad and mom and getting the sense that if we didn't have money, our family would fall apart. I must have been around five years old. I didn't understand what money was, but that day I learned it was something to be afraid of, something if I didn't have enough of – my whole world would disintegrate.

And just like the candidates June counseled, it was not difficult for me to see how I had managed to create a circumstance in my work life that brought out my deepest childhood fears. If I couldn't make placements, if I couldn't make money, my whole world would fall apart. I would end up being deeper in debt, looking stupid in front of all my friends and family and, in general, knowing I was at my very core some kind of loser. Even more than being broke, I hated that idea more than anything else.

On the other hand, if I could make my job with June work, it meant these core beliefs (and the fears that they were constantly generating) were wrong. It meant life wasn't just about survival. It meant money was not something to be feared. More than that, it meant life itself was not something to be feared. It meant I was not a loser but a work in progress. It meant growth was possible. It meant all the bad things that had happened to me in my life were not some kind of judgment or verdict upon the essential 'me', but were just bad things that happened and had no bearing on who I was really was, what I could achieve or what happiness I could experience.

It was with all this on the line that I sat there watching June as she picked up the phone to call my client.

"Hi, may I speak to Crystal?" she asked.

June had her notes from her conversation with Carolyn as well as her application in front of her on her desk.

"Hi, Crystal, this is June Gregory." June had already spoken to Crystal once before when she had presented Carolyn to set up the interview. I found the look on June's face to be very comforting. She looked as though she was talking to her best friend. Her face was radiant, and she was smiling from ear to ear. She was confident, looking as though she was enjoying herself thoroughly.

"I wanted to call and see how the interview went?" June asked.

Before giving Crystal time to answer she interjected, "Isn't she absolutely delightful?"

The next thing I knew June's body was shaking up and down from one of her patented laughs. *This was a good sign*, I thought.

"I thought so as well. She really is delightful. Let me ask you. Did you have any concerns?" June inquired.

Again before Crystal could answer, June interjected, "I spoke to Carolyn after the interview, and she not only loved meeting with you but was very impressed with your organization."

"Good, good, no, I agree. Even though she doesn't have quite as much experience as you would like, she certainly has the maturity and attitude. Let me ask you. Do you think the fact she doesn't quite have the years of experience you like would present a problem?" June asked.

My mind went to *No, June, don't ask that! They might say that 'yes' it is a problem and we won't get the placement!* But as much as June wanted the placement, she wasn't afraid to let go of it if it didn't meet everyone's deepest needs. She genuinely cared more about the integrity of the match than any other factor, the least of which was my overwhelming need to make a placement.

"Yes, I agree. From what I understand you are looking for, I think she would be great, too. That sounds good. I'll give you a chance to touch base with Tom and then we can talk later today. I'd love to hear more about how you manage your office. It sounds like an absolutely fascinating business," June said.

June went on speaking to Crystal a bit longer, but they were no longer talking about Carolyn. When she finally hung up the phone, I asked June why she had brought up the concern about Carolyn's lack of experience.

"Brian, if you are going to learn how to deal well with people, you are going to need to learn how to put their needs before your own. Crystal has a real concern. She's entitled to it. Just because you wish she didn't have it, doesn't make her concern go away."

"But she is perfect for what they are looking for," I insisted.

"You took the job order. I'm reading it right here. It says they wanted a minimum of five years of experience. Carolyn has three and a half at best. If you are going to do this job well you have to keep your objectivity."

My whole being was quickly deflated.

June could see the look of dismay on my face. "Oh, for goodness' sake, if you're going to react to a concern like that, you're never going to make it here. In fact, if that's how you're going to react, you are never going to make it anywhere!"

"It's just I was hoping they would have hired her," I said still feeling the weight of my disappointment.

"If you remember correctly, about two and a half hours ago she wasn't even close to having the confidence to handle the interview, let alone the job. I think she is a good candidate. I liked the way she responded to the challenges I gave her. But she does lack the emotional and professional maturity of a top candidate with more experience," June explained.

I really wasn't hearing too much of what June was trying to tell me. All my insecure mind could comprehend was that Carolyn was not going to get the job offer. I had lost again.

The phone rang, and the call was for June. It was Tom, the president of my client's company. The timing of his call could not have been better for two reasons. First, I had worked with June long enough for me to recognize that the next thing I would have said to June would have really ticked her off. She didn't have a whole lot of tolerance when I got into my "poor me" moods. I would have ended up in the doghouse again, which only would have made things a lot worse between us. Secondly, the fact he was calling and asking for June meant that there still might be hope for a placement.

June collected herself before picking up the phone. She was getting herself focused before talking to Tom.

"Hi, Tom, I'm glad to hear from you. Both Crystal and Carolyn had nothing but great things to say about you." June had completely changed gears. She was back to being her happy, carefree self. She smiled as she continued the conversation.

"Yes, I agree, Carolyn is an unusual candidate. I really think the world of her. What did you think of her?"

I watched as June listened to Tom. She was completely at ease. Her complete concentration was on their conversation.

"I'm glad you liked her and, yes, she is a little light on experience. Let me ask you. How does she compare to the other candidates you have seen so far?"

As June listened she gave me a quick glance. I felt completely helpless just sitting there. But at the same time, it hit me just who I had fighting for me. It had not occurred to me until that moment that June and I were a team. My goodness, if I had been talking to Tom, I would have found 100 different ways to have blown the placement. But June was a master of communication and an expert at making placements. And now she was on the phone with the president, the decision maker. From my perspective, she was fighting as much for me as she was for the placement. Suddenly, there was hope, in fact, the room felt as though it were filled with possibility.

I sat up in my chair as if to root June on. She was listening intently to Tom telling her about the other candidates they were considering.

"Yes, it is difficult to find everything you are looking for in one candidate. The problem I find with hiring the candidate who is asking for more than you really want to pay is, even if you can find some mutual ground, they rarely end up being completely satisfied once they are in the position. It's not a good idea to start a new position already feeling compromised. Those tend not to be the individuals who will give you their best or stay long term."

Wow, what a good point! I thought. I was back to really wanting the placement and believing that June could make it happen. I could tell by the way June was nodding her head that Tom had agreed with her. But the conversation was far from over.

"Your other candidate sounds good. When is she going to get back to you?"

June again nodded and then asked, "How do you feel about the fact that it's taking her so long to get back to you with her answer?"

"Boy, you and I think exactly alike," June said laughing. "If someone doesn't know right away they want to work for me, I keep looking. I don't know if that's my pride or not. However, I can tell you in the best placements I've made, the candidate usually knew right away that they wanted the position. They never needed to think about it. By the way, that's exactly how Carolyn felt when she returned to my office after her interview today."

Whatever Tom said next had June laughing.

"Tom it's important you hire a candidate who has the skills and experience you need. But it's far more important you choose an individual who is dedicated, hard working, takes pride in their work and, most importantly, will add, not distract, from the synergy you have successfully developed in your company. One bad hire, one bad apple can make a difference in the overall performance of a company. Conversely, hiring the right candidate can, as I'm sure you already know, have a very positive impact."

June and Tom spoke for another ten minutes or so. I marveled at how June was counseling the client in much the same manner she counseled the candidates. Tom's company had been growing, which left him less time to help with Human Resource issues. He was afraid if he didn't hire someone with a lot of experience, the good teamwork the company had enjoyed for many years would begin to diminish. June was able to point out to him it was not a matter of experience that was so critical to keeping the teamwork but the attitude of the candidate he hired. Through their conversation Tom was able to see that he, out of his own fear, had been ignoring some of the big red flags that the other candidates had been waving. He thanked June and told her he would like to think about their conversation. He told her he would call her back the next day.

"It's true, Tom, Carolyn does lack some of the experience you would like to have. On the other hand after six months of working for you, she will not only have the experience you are looking for, she will also have the character and attitude it sounds like you want. The problem with your other options is they may start out with the experience, but no matter how long they work for you, it's not likely their character or attitude are going to improve. I want you to end up with everything you want in this hire. If I had a candidate like Carolyn with more experience, I would send her to you. But I don't. I have not seen one in a long time. Candidates with Carolyn's energy and enthusiasm are rare."

I got the impression that Tom was paying attention. June said goodbye and turned her attention back to me.

"June, that was amazing," I told her.

"He really does need someone like Carolyn for that position," she said.

Here I was hoping against all hope that we would make the placement. June, on the other hand, was completely absorbed with Tom's company and making sure that he got the right person.

"Do you think he will make her the offer?" I asked her.

"We'll see," was all she had to say.

On my drive home that evening, there was an unusual amount of traffic. I sat there in my car, not moving, my mind racing as I reviewed the events of the day. The whole day had felt like some strange joyride where all my deepest fears and hopes had been taken out, exposed and batted around. My desire for the placement had revealed to me how much I believed I didn't have what it took to make it in life. The fear had always been there. I just hadn't seen it or felt it has clearly as I had this day. It was such a lousy state of mind, living in this constant fear I was somehow born to lose – I would always be poor, unhappy and uncared for.

On the other hand, I had never experienced such great hope. As I sat there listening to June masterfully talking to Tom about Carolyn, I felt anything was possible. A surge of energy, excitement and confidence ran through my body. With June's help I could be successful. I could have something real to offer the world. And because I had something to offer, I felt positive I would have what it took to make it in life. I hadn't realized it before, but this was the true sense of validation I had been looking for – to have something real to offer. So much of my fear stemmed from this awful feeling I didn't have anything of worth to offer. Nothing to offer, on the one hand, enormous unmet needs on the other. *How could I ever get something, if I had nothing*, I thought. With June's involvement, I was validated. I could have money, be happy and feel cared for.

In this one day, I had seen more clearly than ever before what it meant for me to be unhappy or happy, afraid or encouraged, weak or confident. It was all right there in front of me. And everything was hinging on this one placement. I had to have it.

As my thoughts continued to race, one of my favorite songs came on the radio. The song had a great beat. I turned up the volume, and I found myself singing out loud while beating my hands on the steering wheel. I was so wrapped up in the song that when it ended, I realized the car in front of me was now over 100 yards ahead of me. The driver behind me was honking his horn, trying desperately to get my attention. I can only imagine what the cars on each side of me had been thinking as they watched me hopping up and down in my seat, hitting my steering wheel and singing my heart out. Embarrassed, I hit the gas pedal and quickly caught up to the car in front of me, resuming my proper place in traffic. And that's when it hit me. Maybe I really didn't need the placement.

It was a weird thought at first. It was, in fact, so strange I wondered where it came from. It wasn't like any of my other thoughts – it was a renegade thought. But there it was just sitting there in my mind: *I don't need the placement.* As I mulled over the idea, it started to make more sense. I really didn't need the placement because I had seen what was possible. Hope was possible. Even if I didn't get this placement, I knew without a doubt that with June's guidance I would someday be successful. And making placements meant making money. More than just money, it meant I could grow emotionally and financially at the same time. Life could be good. I didn't have to work just to survive like my dad. I could work to live fully like June. I didn't have to become the person I was afraid of becoming. I could, perhaps, become the person I had always dreamed of.

I was going to have to work for it and it was going to take time, but getting what I truly wanted out of my career was possible. Having a great leader who could help me grow personally and professionally was the key to my new-found belief.

For some reason, I found myself thinking about the story of the three pigs. It occurred to me that I was the third pig. I was building a house of brick. By being in a job where I was growing inwardly as well as financially, I was building something that would last over time. Sure it would take longer, it always takes longer to build a house of brick than one of straw, but the extra time and work would be worth it.

People were laughing at me, just like the third pig, even rejecting me for my choice. But in my gut, I knew that I was doing the right thing. Whether we made the placement or not, I was determined to stick with it. I didn't need the placement because I had already achieved something bigger. I had finally found the faith I had made the right choice. Despite my mounting debt, I was beginning to believe in a future that made sense. Something deep inside my psyche was beginning to change as well. I was beginning to trust.

These brief moments of confidence and trust were just drops of hope in what felt like a vast ocean of fear and insecurity, but they were a beginning – an important one.

The next thing I knew I was pulling up to my house. I was so deep in thought I couldn't remember when or where the traffic had let up.

Before leaving the car, I told myself to remember all the realizations I just had. As ridiculous as it sounds, I was trying to force my mind to remember every detail.

I woke up the next morning feeling unusually good. I couldn't wait to get to the office and begin my recruiting. I laughed when I realized I wasn't even thinking about the possible placement. When I got to work June was on the phone, so I waited for her to get off before I went in to greet her. As soon as she hung up, I went in.

"Good morning, June. I wanted to tell you how much I appreciate what you did yesterday. I was really impressed with the way you spoke with Tom," I said.

I realized I never felt as good about myself as I did during those rare moments when I was telling June that I appreciated her.

"That was Tom I was just talking to," June said.

Suddenly, all my newly discovered detachment disappeared. *I don't need this placement* had been quickly replaced with I WANT THIS!

"What did he say?" I asked, trying to hide my anxiousness.

"He made her the offer," she said.

"He made her the offer." At first it just hung there in the air. "He made her the offer." Did I hear June right? "He made her the offer."

You are not a loser! I thought. *I did it! I did it! I did it!* I thought. Then I went into a state of shock.

I don't remember what, if anything, I said to June. I do remember getting up and leaving to go to the restroom. I was numb. It felt surreal. It was while I was washing my hands that it hit me again. I had helped to make a placement. The candidate was happy. The company was happy. My boss was happy. I was happy. The feeling was amazing. I hadn't realized this was what I had been working so hard for. I thought I had been working for survival. If I had only known how good it would feel to make a placement, I would have worked twice as hard, which wouldn't have been a difficult thing to do.

When I returned to the office, June was on the phone with Carolyn giving her the good news. June was laughing as she listened to Carolyn.

"Hold on a minute, he just got back. Here she would like to talk to you," June said as she handed me the phone.

"Brian, I just want to tell you how grateful I am to you for all the hard work you put into this. I know without your help, this never would have happened. I can't tell you just how excited I am to be working for them. They are such amazing people. I still can't believe that I am going to be working for such an amazing group of people," she said.

As I listened, I knew I didn't deserve her praise. All I had been trying to do was make some money and maybe take care of some of my problems along the way. As I heard the depth of Carolyn's appreciation, the joy of making the placement began to increase even further. Carolyn would now be working for the kind of people she had always wanted to work for but could never seem to find. The client had found exactly the caliber of candidate they had been looking for but were having difficulty attracting.

And then there was me. I had just earned my first income as a headhunter. In the process, I had helped a person and a company. It was a win–win–win situation. Everyone involved had benefited. Ironically, I was so thrilled about placing Carolyn I didn't even know, or particularly care, how much money I had made. All I could think about was this new amazing sensation called a placement!

When I arrived home I tried to explain my excitement to my wife and anyone else who would listen. I called everyone I knew. "I made a placement! You see, the candidate went from a negative environment to a positive one, all because I called her! Our client got a great new employee who will be a key to their growth because I cold called them! Do you understand the company and the candidate are both better off because of my efforts? Isn't that awesome! And I'm getting paid! I'm making money for this!" I went on and on about the placement, boring everyone who would listen.

I had trouble sleeping that night. Suddenly, I was in love with my job! I couldn't wait to make the next placement and then the next. That's when another realization hit me. Work could be fun. Making money could be fun. You could make a positive impact on other peoples' lives while improving your own at the same time. Sure, there was hard work involved, but this feeling was worth it. I had been working toward a goal with absolutely no idea of the reason for my efforts or the satisfaction of the accomplishment. I had been just trying to survive – to pay my bills. I knew that, besides just trying to earn some money, I was working for a very unusual boss who had been more honest with me than anyone I had ever met. But I had no idea that the payoff would result in such an inexplicable feeling of freedom and happiness.

As I lay in bed thinking, I remember wishing that my family and friends could experience what it was like to make a placement. If they could only know how great it felt, they would have done everything in their power to encourage me in my new job with June. They never would have tried so hard to talk me out of it. And then it occurred to me maybe that was the real problem. They could not support me because they had never known what I was now experiencing. They had not known what it felt like to take a financial risk – or any risk – to work for someone they truly admired in a field they knew nothing about. They didn't know what it was like to truly win: to go up against your worst fears and to come out the other side feeling stronger and better about yourself. They didn't know the joy that came from seeing someone else benefit as a direct result of their own growth. They didn't know the amazing feeling of happiness that came with risking everything based only on a hunch and then discovering that hunch was the best choice they had ever made. My family and friends were in no position to encourage me because they had never known work to be so deeply meaningful or joyful. Like me, they had not known the incredible benefits that could come from taking risks.

Just like June's example of a penny in and a penny out, junk in and junk out also applies, I thought. If I go to someone who is unhappy in their work life for advice, they will give me advice that fits their experience and perceptions. Everyone advises from their own vantage point. If I want to continue to experience this great feeling, then I must from now on only go for advice to someone who knows this feeling. Since June was the only one I had ever met who understood what I was experiencing, I knew I needed to continue to go to her and, at least for now, only her for direction.

For the first time in as long as I could remember, I fell asleep that night free from all my fears, anxieties and stress. I was happy. I felt like I was being put back together after twenty-three years of being slowly pulled apart.

Put back together again by my boss June.

Your Right Job, Right Now

That's the story of my first placement. I will tell you the rest of the story in another book. Until then, let me leave you with a few thoughts.

First, we are all far more alike than we are different. At our core, we all have the same desires in our career: to have a deep sense of purpose, to be led by a person we trust and admire, to live fully and to make a positive impact on the lives of others. Not only do we have the same desires, but we are also caught up in the same web of lies. We live in a world that is constantly sending us messages that we are what we do, we are what we have and we are what other people think of us. Once we recognize these lies, we want to break free, but we're just not sure how to do it. It feels so overwhelming, doesn't it? What specific actions do I really need to take to have the life I want?

Because we are more alike than we are different, the answers in my story are applicable to your story. We all start out with a dream. I wanted to be Spiderman. Do you remember the excitement of your first dream? Mine was lost at age five. Do you remember when you lost yours? As the years went by, I fell into a pit of inadequacy, fear, and worry. I created a "false self", a front to cover my fears and inadequacy. I suspect you did the same. By the time I turned 23, I hit rock bottom. Out of pure desperation, I prayed (for the first time in my life) for what I really wanted—someone who would bring out the best in me. You've certainly experienced some low moments of your own and probably reached out for help as well.

My prayer was answered in the form of a five-foot, two-hundred-pound former torch singer. It was answered, not in the form of a job, or income or title, but in the form of a person. Once it was answered, I had to learn how to accept the exact opposite of what I thought I wanted. To top it all off, I had to face the reality of my worst fear: becoming a "broke idiot".

Are you willing to face your worst fears? Are you willing to break completely free from lies and false associations that are holding you back? Are you willing to take risks to become the person you know you were meant to be?

Secondly, we are alike in our weaknesses. We all have these "big uglies" which are actions, thoughts and choices that, we are convinced, would disqualify us from being the people we want to be. Most of us have gotten good at covering up the truth about our fears and inadequacies. We choose to work for leaders that have us living more in our weaknesses than our power. We live far more in our fear than our courage. We have good days and bad, but in the final analysis, we sense there is something more important, something deep inside of us, that is missing in our lives and our careers.

That's why we need people like June. Someone who sees the best in us and is bold enough to help us fight to achieve it; who is both courageous and loving; who will call us out on our lies, fears and inadequacies.

June's mission was to help people find their own best person. I invite you to keep referring to this book until you do too.

As she often asked her candidates: "how do you know you can't find that person until you have really tried; until you have given it everything you've got?" Giving up on that quest is giving up on yourself. I can tell you that once you find THAT "you", the nagging sense that something is missing in your career will disappear.

In my twenty-five years of experience, I don't believe I ever met a person genuinely willing to make the choices June spells out in this book, who did not go on to work for a better leader. Now, more than ever, we need to make those choices. Because of the changes in the job market, the days of compromise are over. We will need to bring our best to find the jobs we want. And if we want to be great (as a person, or as a company or even as a people) we need to bring our best to the best leaders. That is the key to rebuilding ourselves and our communities.

In the movie *Starman*, Jeff Bridges plays an alien who is visiting earth. He tells us he has visited many species across the Universe, and at one point in the movie he states, "May I tell you what I find most beautiful about your species? **You are at your best when things are at their worst.**"

He's right. We are all capable of being our best when things are at their worst. The time to do that is now.

When we are bold enough to follow what we know in our hearts, minds and souls to be true, we will discover a new job market. A market where we will find jobs so good, so clearly designed just for us, that we will find ourselves overwhelmed with gratitude for the right job, right now.

"Let go of your fears and doubts. Then you become free to bring your best self, your true self to the interview."
June Gregory

Epilogue

Twenty-five Years Later: Life after June (It's Really Not that Complicated)

I looked at my calendar, half hoping I was wrong.

My first wife and I divorced after four years of marriage. I waited 19 years before finding my second wife, Kim. She tells people that God literally dropped me on her doorstep. And she was right.

Kim is the founder and executive director of an urban ministry in the Bay Area that supports emancipated foster youths who age out of the system at 18 and have no place to go, no money and no emotional support. If not helped, a high percentage of these young women end up homeless, pregnant, in prostitution, or even worse, dead. My wife's program, named Jeremiah's Promise, offers a home, mentoring, educational support, life skills classes and therapeutic and career counseling. Jeremiah's Promise is a unique program in that it offers the girls the same type of ongoing positive involvement that June had so unselfishly given to me. Also like June, part of the program's success is based on the idea that the girls are not just given handouts. In exchange for a home and other assistance, they agree to complete high school and then enter college, work part-time, and save money so they can eventually afford a place of their own. They also must perform volunteer service to give back to the community that is giving to them. It's no surprise that given the level of positive and comprehensive involvement with each girl, the program is successful in transforming the lives of these youth.

It's also no small wonder that I fell in love with the woman who founded it. Kim embodies the same fierce commitment to love complete strangers that June had. Like June, she's not afraid to say or do the difficult thing that would send most of us running for our comfort zones. But before you think me too emotionally mature, I have a confession: this woman is a total knockout!

As I looked at my calendar again, a smile spread over my face. It had been 25 years to the day since I first met June. More than four years had gone by since the day I was at her side when she passed away. I missed my boss very much.

Although she was gone, the influence she has on my life is far from over. In fact, if anything, it has intensified! In the last four years, I met and married the woman of my dreams and started my own search firm, continuing June's legacy. My daughter Jessy was my star employee. My brother Rob (the child of my dad's second marriage!) is the best friend I could ever hope for. And because of the surprising success of my business, I am able to devote some of my time and financial resources to helping organizations such as Jeremiah's Promise.

My life now could not be more different from the life of the lost soul who first wandered into June's office. I have achieved success in both my professional and personal life beyond my wildest imagination. In fact, most days I wake up wondering if it was all just a dream. With a sense of complete awe I find myself wondering, "How did I get here? How did all these great things happen to me, the guy who was supposed to be such a loser?"

Someone once said that there are two great joys in life. One is the joy of *intimacy*. If we choose well, we experience joy in our personal lives. The other is the joy of *accomplishment*. Again, if we choose well, we experience joy in our work lives. Thanks to my boss June, who spent more than 20 years kicking my butt until she had made me into the man I was designed to be, I am now experiencing both of these great joys to the full. More than 20 years of involvement has meant a cycle of growing, regressing, then growing again, trusting and mistrusting, then trusting again. Through her tremendous capacity to love and her immense courage she has helped transform me. I was now more like her than my parents. What a legacy! One woman, a stranger who was an answer to my first and simplest of prayers: "God please help me. Please bring me a person who will bring out the very best in me. I want to become my very best. I know it's in there."

And He did. As Francis Frangipane said, "Rescue is the constant pattern of God's activity."

He brought me my boss June. Every joy, every ounce of success I now enjoyed was a testimony to God's constant pursuit of me through this remarkable woman.

But the "best in me" I prayed for was far more than the success I was now enjoying. June taught me how to be strong. Over the years, I watched as she dealt with three close calls with death. She was betrayed several times by people she trusted and held very dear. She experienced financial loss, the death of two of her sisters and she spent more than a year going through the agonizing process of dialysis. She was unbelievably strong, yet she was able to weep when others couldn't. She was courageous when others succumbed to fear. She was the first to admit her weaknesses, yet she didn't let anything or anyone stop her. And she was the first to step in to help others. She lived life to the full. She experienced all its passions, joys and beauty. She also experienced all its heartache, pain and tragedy. She lived without compromise.

June taught me that the "best in me" is far more than what I do, what I have or what other people think of me. It is that place within me that knows truth versus lies and chooses the truth no matter the cost. It knows giving from taking and chooses to give especially when it is difficult. It knows courage from fear and chooses to be courageous even when it may cost everything. It knows love from self-interest and chooses love even as the whole world laughs.

Everything June did for me, she did to bring out the best in me. Other than giving your life for another, I wonder if there is any greater form of love.

Before I met June I had nothing. I lacked character, strength, money, self-respect or self-esteem. I was incapable of loving myself or others. Yet, the moment I met her, I had the means to fulfill every one of my passions, dreams and desires. I had nothing, but I had everything. That is the power of having an exceptional boss. That is the importance of relationship in our lives.

June taught me when we can learn to see the setbacks, disappointments and even the successes in our careers as opportunities to grow, then we can begin to see how our careers are actually a constant process of rescue from our fears, stresses and unhappiness. We can also begin to see how our circumstances are always giving us an opportunity to choose to move closer to realizing our dreams and deepest desires.

The second most important thing I've learned about our careers is we *need other people to accurately interpret our circumstances.* No one, I repeat, no one can accurately interpret the circumstances of their work life without the help of someone else. That's the design. And that's why who you choose to be that person will have a more profound effect on your career than any other single factor including education, dedication, hard work, intelligence, good intentions, who you know, what you know, what you earn, how well-liked or respected you are, etc, etc.

As I studied my calendar and ended my reverie, I saw I hadn't been mistaken. Today was the day I was scheduled to go to Jeremiah's Promise and offer career counseling to two young women. As I got in my car, I started thinking about what I wanted to tell them. I knew both of these girls had experienced more abuse and rejection in their young lives than most of us could ever imagine – me included. I knew it would be very difficult to help them connect to their dreams and desires. The more wounds we suffer early in life, the more difficult it is to allow ourselves to dream about what we desire most. At the same time, they had nothing to lose. They had experienced some of the worst life had to offer, and they still chose to live at Jeremiah's Promise because they hadn't given up on life or themselves. They could have chosen other options that would have asked far less of them than this program.

I came to the conclusion that these two young ladies had components of career growth that I was looking for. They wanted to grow, and they had nothing to lose. But, on the other hand, I knew that they weren't about to listen to me talk to them about career growth. The small flame of hope that brought them to Jeremiah's Promise would not survive my blustery diatribe on job hunting. So how could I get them to understand what I wanted to tell them about their careers?

As it had so many times before, the answer came to me during my drive. I knew they were going to shut down the moment I started telling them what to do. So I decided I wasn't going to tell them what to do. I was going to let them tell me.

Susan, the Education and Career Specialist at Jeremiah's Promise, met me at the door when I arrived. She introduced me to the girls and explained to them that I was there to help them with their careers. Both of the girls looked up at me as if I was there to try to sell them a time-share. It occurred to me that career counseling for an 18-year-old is about as exciting as getting a tooth pulled. Nevertheless, Susan, the two girls and I sat down at the kitchen table to talk.

"Brian, would you like to tell the girls a little bit about career counseling?" Susan asked politely.

I looked at Mary and Heidi. They were both sitting with their shoulders slumped, their eyes cast downward.

"I don't know anything about it. I just got fired from my crappy job!" I said with as much of a lousy attitude as I could muster, my shoulders slumped, my eyes looking down at the table. I was mirroring their demeanor.

Jolted, the two girls looked up. Their eyes opened wide with their shoulders back against their chairs.

"That same thing happened to me!" Mary said.

"It did?"

'Uh, huh. I was working for a pet shop because I love animals. I was late so many times I guess they had to fire me. What did they get you for?"

"I don't know and don't care," I said.

"That's a really bad attitude. If you want the people you work for to treat you well, you can't be going around like that," Mary interjected.

"That's right," Heidi added.

"Oh, and I guess you two never have bad attitudes at work. I doubt that. Besides I didn't ask you for advice."

"Well, you sure sound like you need it!" Mary said.

"Well, what am I supposed to do? The job was boring and the people were stupid."

"Hey, you're the one who picked them. Nobody made you take it," Heidi started shaking her head in righteous indignation.

"Oh, so you're saying I'm responsible for the job I take and the people I choose to work for?"

"That's right. You're not some kind of victim. You need to get over yourself," Mary said.

"Okay, maybe you're right. I should be writing down these ideas. Can you take notes for me?" I asked Mary.

"Sure," she said. Susan handed her some paper and a pen. "Don't be some kind of victim and get over your sorry self," she said, writing as she spoke.

"Well how am I supposed to know what the people are like by just going on one or two interviews?" I asked.

"You've got to look for nice people. Don't you know whether people are nice or not? It's not hard to tell." Heidi was looking at me as though she was trying to figure out why I was so stupid.

"It's not that easy. Sometimes mean people act nice on an interview," I said.

"You have to pay attention to the way they shake your hand and how they look at you. If you pay attention, it's really easy," Heidi insisted.

"Yeah, the friendly ones are friendly, and the mean ones are mean. You can tell when they're faking it. You just have to listen to what your insides are telling you," Mary added.

"Okay, write that one down for me too."

"Yeah, that's a good one. You've got to pay attention or you're dead! One time I worked for these people, but as soon as I saw the way they were treating the other girls, I was out of there," Mary said.

"You just quit?" I asked.

"Right there on the spot. I just got my things and walked out," she said proudly.

"So you're saying that if I find out the people aren't nice that I should just leave?"

"That's what I do. You can do what you want. But if I were you I wouldn't let myself be messed with," she added with an attitude of her own.

"Okay, that's another one. Write it down on the list," I said.

"That's right, don't take no crap. There's always another job out there if you work hard enough to find it," Mary stated emphatically.

"Write that down, too," I said.

"You're messed up. Write *that* down and put it at the top of the page!" Heidi said.

The two enjoyed a good laugh and gave each other a high-five. "I think he needs a Zoloft," Heidi added.

It took everything I had not to burst out laughing. I thought June had been tough. These two were bringing a whole new dimension to career counseling.

"No kidding, I just got fired. You would be messed up too if you just lost your job," I said.

"You got to start looking for a new one and stop feeling sorry for yourself," Heidi insisted.

"What's the point? I'll probably just end up finding another job like the one I just had."

"You're paranoid. *Paranoia will destroy ya!* You've got to have good thoughts about your future, or you might as well just give up now," Mary said.

"What do you mean by 'good thoughts'?'?" I asked

"You know. What do you want to be? Goals, stuff like that," Mary said.

"Like what? What are your goals?"

Mary looked perplexed, "I don't know. I guess I don't have any."

"That's great! You're telling me to have some goals, and you don't even have any yourself!"

"Well, I'd like to go to college and maybe work with animals," she said very softly.

"Oh, then you do have a goal."

Mary looked up at me as if I had told her that she had just won the lottery. "Yeah, I do have one! I want to go to school. Then I want to work with animals!"

"Are you just trying to make me feel bad because you have a dream and I don't have one?" I asked.

"Oh, no! I'll help you find one," she said.

"How?"

"Well, what do you like to do?"

"I like helping people," I said.

"Then you should do that! That's your goal!"

"I think you should go to school or something first. Right now, I don't think you'd be very good at helping anyone," Heidi interjected.

"If you work on it, though, you could learn!" Mary said, trying to encourage me.

"Yeah, I suppose so," I replied. "Let me ask you another question. Let's say I take all the advice you have given me and I find a job I really like. Then one day I wake up and I'm in a really lousy mood. What am I supposed to do with that?"

"You have to fake it," Heidi responded.

"What do you mean?"

"If you want to work for nice people in a job you really like, you have to learn to act nice even when you don't feel like it. I'm an expert at that because I like acting."

"Isn't that called 'being a phony'?"

"No, it's called 'keeping a job'."

Susan indicated to me our time was coming to a close. I could see Mary was beginning to be genuinely concerned for my welfare, so I knew it was time to end the charade and come clean with the girls.

"Okay, speaking of being a phony, I have to tell you I really didn't lose my job today. I just made that up because I knew if I came over here and lectured you on career counseling you would have been bored."

"You got that right!" Heidi said.

"And do you know why you would have been bored?" I asked.

"Wait, you really have a job?" Mary asked, completely confounded.

"Yes, I run a search firm where I do career counseling."

"That's what Kim's husband does," Mary said.

"I am Kim's husband."

"Oh! Now I get it! Wow, I'm glad you have a job. To be honest, I was really worried about you."

"Thank you, Mary, I appreciate that. But do you know why you would have been bored?"

"Because we already know the answers?" she asked.

"Yep, you already know everything there is to know."

"And we haven't even been through college!" Mary exclaimed.

"Well, I have to tell you. It's one thing to know how to do the right thing and a whole other thing to actually do it."

"Wait, if you're Kim's husband, you were writing a book on how to find a job or something, right?"

Mary was still recovering from the fact that I wasn't out of work.

"Yes, that's right."

"How come you didn't tell us about the book?"

"Would you like to read it?"

"Depends, what's it about?'

"It's about the woman I worked for most of my life. She helped me and many other people get over themselves. Once they got over themselves, she was a master at helping them live their dreams. The book is about the first year I worked for her."

"What happened to her?"

"She passed away about four years ago. I think about her every day."

"I'd like to read it. I know a lot of people I would like to see get over their fancy selves," Mary said.

"I would like to read about her, too. Did she live her dreams?" Heidi asked.

"More than anyone else I have ever known. But it wasn't easy. She was very brave."

"What about all those other years you worked for her? Are you going to write about that too?" Heidi asked.

"Yes, someday I'll write a book about those other years."

"It sounds like an interesting story," Mary said.

"It is," I said smiling.

All My Years of Career Counseling Summed Up by Mary and Heidi

1. You're responsible for the people you choose to work for.
2. Get over your sorry self.
3. Don't be a victim.
4. Listen to what your insides are telling you: friendly people are friendly and mean people are mean.
5. Don't take no crap.
6. Have goals and good thoughts about your future: Paranoia Will Destroy Ya!
7. If you are having a bad day (while working for good people), fake it. Be nice! It's called keeping a job.
8. You already know all the answers. It's doing it that's the hard part.

We'd like to hear your stories about how *Your Right Job, Right Now* has influenced you. Also, to purchase a *Your Right Job, Right Now* workbook or to find out about workshops go to **www.mybossjune.com**.